FOR T. A. LAWRENCE, –
DISTINGUISHED MEMBER OF THE
CANADIAN AVIATION
HALL OF FAME.

## OPEN GANGWAY

Cheers !

Stanley R. Redman

# OPEN GANGWAY

## The (Real) Story
## Of The Halifax Navy Riot

by

**Stanley R. Redman**

LANCELOT PRESS

Hantsport, Nova Scotia

ISBN  0-88999-150-2

Published 1981
  Second Printing January 1982
  Third Printing September 1983
  Fourth printing January, 1985
  Fifth printing June 1986

LANCELOT PRESS LIMITED, Hantsport, N. S.
Office and plant situated on Highway No. 1, 1/2 mile east of Hantsport

# DEDICATED TO

My wife, Helen, who put up with my incessant typing in various bed-sitters in Wartime Halifax; who joins with me in pleasant recollection of the Haligonian hospitality we were accorded.

With drunken joy riders at the controls, this streetcar jumped the rails on Barrington Street. A shore patrol wagon that gave chase was stopped by a hail of bottles.

# CONTENTS

As a shore patrolman looks the other way, the mob raids Keith's brewery.

8

# Chapter 1
# THE SECRET MEMO —
# "TO APPREHEND A RATING"

"My God!" said Desk Sergeant Charles White, as he leaned back in his swivel chair, yawning. "Things are dead! Nothing like 1918 when they tried to burn the City Hall." He looked up at the clock. Three quarters of an hour till midnight. Time then to change the calendar from May 7th.

Three minutes later the phone rang stridently and he came wide awake with a report that a tram was on fire on Barrington Street, set ablaze, it was said, by a mob of sailors celebrating. Victory time in Halifax, in 1945, was to be the first occasion since the Rebellion of 1837 that lawful authorities would be so massively defied. But, whereas, in the early year of the new Queen Victoria's reign, Sir Francis Bond Head's military commanders flung themselves against the insurgents and routed them, Mayor Allan M. Butler was not to be so well served. Hesitating to invoke Martial Law for fear of bloodshed and then finding it was not even his prerogative, he spent the crucial hours conferring with the vacillating local heads of the Armed Services and Royal Canadian Mounted Police. By then it was too late for action to spare the city from a destruction no less complete than had the Germans landed.

It was the start of a chain of events which would see thousands of naval ratings and petty officers, largely without hindrance, attack the historic city which had welcomed them, and which had been proud to call itself a "Navy Town", with

9

barely a nod to the "Junior Services", the Army and the Royal Canadian Air Force. The tars would tax the hospitals and jails and cause losses and damage which even today would be substantial, but in that era amounted to a staggering $5,000,000.

They would fuel the unfortunate flames of regionalism; bring contempt for Halifax from those who lived outside it, and bitter resentment by Haligonians for "Upper Canadians" and that more remote but almost equally distasteful breed of lawless land-locked Westerners, who seemed to have contributed an inordinate percentage of deep sea sailors. These results, and much more, would spring from the glacial dignity and incompetence of one man, Rear-Admiral Leonard Warren Murray, C.B. C.B.E., Commander-in-Chief North West Atlantic. He was a man who suffered neither fools nor civilians gladly, the kind of senior officer his subordinates would hesitate to disturb with unwelcome news.

By September of the previous year, the Allies were firmly established on the continent and a U.S. army under General Alexander Patch had landed in the south of France. Bulgaria had capitulated and Roumania had not only accepted armistice but had declared war on the Reich. At the Dumbarton Oaks Conference the U.S.A., Great Britain and Russia were already discussing proposals for a post-war international organization. Paris and Brussels had been liberated and, at Quebec, President Roosevelt and Prime Minister Churchill were drawing up their blueprints for a world at peace.

With the cessation of hostilities just over the horizon, it was good civic planning when the then Mayor, J.E. Lloyd, called a meeting to enquire into what protection the armed services could give to Halifax and Dartmouth, its across-the-harbour neighbour, to prevent rowdyism and damage in victory celebrations. Civilians and representatives of the forces were present to give their opinions on this important subject.

It was agreed that the heads of the service police would meet privately with the Halifax Chief of Police and all would keep their masters informed. Following a meeting of the "Sub-Committee Administrative of the Joint Services Committee,

Atlantic Coast", the minutes read, in part; "The representatives of the armed services left the civic authorties at this meeting with the impression that the projected parade would be purely a civic affair with the Armed Services co-operating in controlling troops and policing main points of the city for the purpose of maintaining order amongst service personnel. Special precautions would be taken to prevent any attempt being made by service personnel to break into liquor vendors."

When Admiral Murray was later advised that the stores of the Nova Scotia Liquor Commission would be closed and it had been suggested that the wet canteens might follow suit, he replied that the matter had been discussed with the other two services. In their view it would be better that the canteens remain open to the extent of the limited supplies available on that day. His letter went on to say: "retention of the canteens under proper control, will go a long way towards keeping crowds of Service personnel off the streets where they might do harm to private and public property...This, combined with an organization to set up sing-songs and entertainments should go a long way to relieve the impact of large numbers of joyful service personnel upon the city."

McCurdy Printing of Halifax was duly authorized to produce a quantity of program sheets for distribution on V-E Day as the happy event had by then been named.

## ORDER OF SERVICE

### O CANADA!
Ending with the lines;
"As waiting for the Better Day
We ever stand on guard."

ADDRESS: By the Commander-in-Chief
Canadian North West Atlantic

HYMN: "O God Our Help In Ages Past"

LESSON: PSALM 46, District Officer Commanding M.D.6

### PRAYERS

The Sub-Committee concurred and declared that "this would encourage personnel to remain in camp and less likely to congregate in unruly gangs downtown and could, therefore, be the means of extended control."

At a naval meeting in Ottawa, attended by Lt. Commander Reginald Wood, the Shore Patrol Officer in the Halifax area, the 'top brass' decided, in its wisdom, "that naval patrols should not appear on the streets, but should be held in reserve to answer calls of an emergency nature in the case of Possible Disorders."

What little was known of defensive preparations did nothing to allay a feeling of unease held by the Halifax North Civic Improvement Association, a group of citizens living nearby large naval establishments where they had had the opportunity to observe conditions prevailing on Navy Pay Days. Noting that while "there would undoubtedly be great rejoicing and jubilation," they felt obliged to resolve that; 'Whereas some of the people who will then be in this city are likely to celebrate said day in a riotous and rowdy manner and to molest peaceful citizens and damage and destroy their property.

'And Whereas breaches of the peace and damage and destruction of property are most likely to occur in restaurants, tea rooms and theatres and other public places. And Whereas it is imperative that all necessary steps be taken by the responsible authorities to preserve order and to protect the persons and property of the citizens of Halifax on that day and in particular that adequate police protection be provided for that purpose on said day.....earnestly urge the responsible authorities to take the necessary steps . . . etc., etc.' "

The Resolution came onto Admiral Murray's paper-laden desk in due course but, as it "contained nothing which he did not at that time have in mind already," it was consigned to File 13.

12

Near the end of April, Mussolini's body hung upside down, along with that of his mistress, Clara Petacci, in Milan's Square of *Quindici Martiri,* from the girder of a service station. And, on the last day, Hitler came to his end in a bunker of the Chancellory in Berlin. History unrolled at a furious rate; but, for the citizens of Halifax who had seen their birthplace taken over by 30,000 uniforms and in many cases the wives or camp followers, the waiting seemed prolonged beyond all endurance.

For years they had been forced to listen to the foreign accents of Upper Canadians and those further West, raised in a litany of criticism on which there was little brake to diminish the volubility or to soften the galling jeers. The beloved trams, they were told, were ridiculous little 'Toonerville Trollies'. "In Tranna, you step on the treadle and the doors open!" The largely unwanted 'visitors' had few inhibitions about commenting on the lack of night or any other kind of life, the gouging rents paid by those so fortunate as to find a room, the meagre allotment of one bottle of liquor per person per month; in short, the bountiful amenities which they had enjoyed at home — in peace time.

Servicemen spent their off-duty hours wandering aimlessly about the streets or queuing for the one large downtown theatre, The Capitol; the handful of restaurants, the Green Lantern, Lohnes... which were always jammed; the overworked laundries which kept their shirts for ever. They could get buttons or badges sewed on at the Sally Ann or the K of C; they could get, for twenty cents at the Wings Club in the Nova Scotian Hotel, a glass of milk and the world's biggest toasted egg salad sandwich. But there were no open beverage rooms in town and the only girls they were likely to get close to were the tarts on Water or Hollis Streets. After the first great rash of teenage pregnancies, parents kept their daughters under unrelenting vigil. Aside from those vital things, they were sick and tired of the war, for the most part, and considered themselves exiled near the *maximus cloaca* of the Dominion, where their presence was bitterly resented by Maritimers in general and Haligonians in particular.

Both residents and reluctant guests were subjected,

13

almost hourly, to fresh rumours soon to be deflated, that the end had come. While obviously not as nerve-wracking as their counterparts across the Atlantic who could expect Blockbusters or V-Bombs at any moment, those in the "Eastern Canadian Seaport" lacked the immediacy of war to give them the stoical acceptance of whatever should befall.

It had been common knowledge, for at least the previous year, that the end of the war in Europe would be a "rough day for Halifax!" There were persistent rumours that some sort of vengeance would be extracted by the Navy. Red-coated Corporal Newman MacLean would profess to believe this was a prediction of a "rough time for the police in keeping traffic moving, handling crowds and so forth." Out-of-province sailors were dissatisfied with Halifax, its people and the area in general. Five hundred times in a twelve month period, Conductor Michael Dwyer had heard them complain about the weather and "the damned trams", their dislike of the local Oland's Moosehead beer supplied to canteens instead of Quebec beer more to their taste. The majority had acquired neither taste for nor tolerance to hard liquor, almost entirely reserved for the delectation of officers. "What a bum town this is!", they snarled. "What a place to be dumped in! We'll take Halifax apart!"

In considering the possibility that they might be so tempted when the glorious day dawned, Lt. Cmdr. Wood issued a memo to his shore patrol crews, to be memorized and destroyed. The substance of this mysterious instruction was that success would rely on tact and persuasion rather than force. Or, as Admiral Murray would put it; "The intention was to lead, as with a child, instead of saying 'Don't do that.' " And, as Wood cautioned his men, "If the patrol see damage being done, it was to stop it if possible, but to take no further action." Wood felt, and the Admiral concurred, that to apprehend a rating on such a day might provoke a serious riot. Not, as might have been expected, by his mates but by civilians seeing their brave protectors chastised.

The use of jeeps was to be terminated as, being light small vehicles, it would be simple to turn them over, and to do so might be considered a joke. Admiral Murray did not wish the Shore Patrol to be exposed to such low humour but, above all, there must be no degredation of the majesty of the law which it represented. His mind and time were more exercised with protecting secret and costly stores intended for the war against Japan. He issued general instructions to his officers to padlock ammunition lockers and magazines, to look to their depth charges and pyrotechnics. Perhaps as an afterthought, he suggested that gangways and 'scramble nets' be arranged adequate to prevent men falling over the sides "in case they should return in semi-inebriated condition".

To anxious Mayor Butler, Civil Defence Director Major O.R. Crowell and Halifax Police Chief Judson J. Conrod, the strength available to handle fractious servicemen was detailed as: 200 Naval Shore Patrol, 150 Army Provost Corps, and 60 to 75 RCAF Special Police. With 83 Halifax policemen and several dozen Mounties to look after civilians, the situation was surely well in hand.

On May 2nd, Soviet armies forced the surrender of Berlin. Although isolated tough resistance continued, within 48 hours German armies in Holland, Denmark and northwest Germany itself capitulated and on May 6th the Nazi forces in Austria bowed to the inevitable. On Monday the 7th, in the city of Reims at 2:41 French time, which was 8:41 Eastern War Time it was all over. Admiral Murray received official but secret word at 0500, about five hours before the Associated Press dispatch that slipped through European censorship. At 10:30 a.m. in Halifax, the whistles began to blow on the navy vessels in the great harbour and all civilians who could do so ran out into the streets.

# Chapter 2
# A CELEBRATION GETTING OUT OF HAND

Mayor Butler hastened to proclaim the following day, Tuesday, May 8th, as V-E Day, inviting all citizens to Thanksgiving Services at 2:30 p.m. on the Garrison Grounds. Provision would be made, he said, for community singing, demonstrations and celebrations; there would be dancing on South Park Street, from Sackville to Spring Garden Road. He requested all to refrain from creating pedestrian congestion in the down-town area. Finally, he reminded them that "VICTORY IN EUROPE IS NOT FINAL VICTORY".

Although the display of fireworks had originally been scheduled as the culmination of V-E Day itself, it seemed a pity to delay them that long and, as well, it would provide a spectacle to occupy people's minds, thus avoiding undue and premature exuberance. Consequently, it had been decided to alter the program and set off the extravaganza on Monday night instead. Admiral Murray was notified, as were the other Commanding Officers whose cooperation was said to be forthcoming, although no one quite knew of what it consisted.

A crowd of nearly 15,000 had congregated that night on the eastern slope of Citadel Hill and, as the weather was mild, it was no hardship to spend a few hours until darkness would do full justice to the scene. In due course, and perhaps not easy to come by with wartime shortages, a number of sky rockets were seen soaring up over the great harbour where they could be viewed by celebrants on both shores.

There were ooohs and aaahs from the children who were too young to have seen such a sight before and, as might have been expected, a chorus of loud untactful tributes from Upper Canadians for whom the Canadian National Exhibition spectacle was the *sine qua non* by which others should be judged. However, as the last starburst expired and the final miniature comet fizzled into the water, it was a good-natured mixed crowd of civilians and service people who left the hill and dispersed homeward, glad that it was all over (Little did they know!)

The normal hours for a soldier to be back at his barrack, unless with a night pass, ranged from 10:15 to 11:45 depending on the orders of the unit to which he belonged. Airforce regulations were similar but the Navy practice was quite different. For reasons never established, but possibly because it was the Senior Service and entitled to such privileges, all naval personnel not on duty were free from 5:00 p.m. till 7:00 a.m. the following day. All, that is, except for those in their teens. It is not to be wondered at then that those in uniform that night in Halifax, some thousands of them, were almost all from His Majesty's Canadian Ships Scotian, Stadacona, Peregrine, as the shore establishments were named. Meanwhile, approximately 4,000 soldiers and C.W.A.C were bedded down in their respective lights-out barracks, as were about 300 Women's Division lower ranks of the RCAF. On the Dartmouth shore, at Eastern Passage, the 1,600 airmen and a handful of W.D.'s were safely inside their compound with lights out. Meanwhile, many thousands of naval ratings from shore establishments and ships in the harbour were free to wander, unchecked, through the hours of the night.

Tram Car no.126 was destined to go down in history as a martyr among its fellows, from the indignities heaped on its aged person. As it creaked along south on Barrington Street about 10:30 p.m. its blue-coated passengers ejected the operator and took over. The street was choked with naval personnel who shattered windows missed by those inside who had then turned to uprooting the ancient scuffed seats. Several hundred ratings attempted to overturn it but, although they

17

got it rocking, no. 126 refused to topple. Enraged by this show of dumb resistance, a number of them lit newspapers and started fires amongst the wreckage of the seats. Police Sgt. Verdun W. Mitchell, along with Sgt. Malay, Constable Dickson and others, managed to keep these under control but the tars were a resourceful lot. One of them, probably a knowledgeable Engine Room Artificer, pried open a journal box and set fire to the oily waste. Great flaming bunches tossed into the car's interior drove out the police who managed to send a distress call. A police cruiser buffeted its way through the dense yelling crowd, but when it could go no further it soon found itself on its side. The indignant reinforcements were lucky to escape, for when its gas tank ruptured a sailor flung a cigarette into the spreading gasoline. With a great WHOOM, a pillar of fire leaped up into the sky. A tank veteran would have called it a fine 'brew-up'!

Over the roar of the crowd, sirens could be heard and the clang of bells as Deputy Fire Chief Joseph William Harber and his almost brand new $24,000 pumper proudly arrived on the scene. Twice the firemen laid down the hoses which were promptly disconnected at the hydrants by some of the sailors. But when they ripped the fire axes from his pumper and began to hack the hose to pieces, Harber realized that the tone of the celebrations had gone from what might have been charitably described as riotous good humour to an ugly mood, and it was not likely to improve. When he was warned that he had better take off or his equipment would be upset, he could do nothing else. And the ten policemen there could do nothing for him.

It had been reported to Lt. Cmdr. Wood by Warrant Officer Barbour that the latter had already sent two trucks with thirty shore patrolmen, but they had been attacked and driven off when burning paper and rags were thrown onto the canvas tops of their vehicles. Wood rushed to the fiery scene and found 15 Shore Patrol there but they were doing nothing as "there was nothing they could do."

As for the burned out patrol wagon, when it was cool enough to handle, it was righted and energetic ratings pushed it off down the street toward the harbour, into the water of which it would surely have plunged had the pushers not thought of a

18

more profitable diversion. It was abandoned on one of the docks, a complete write-off.

While no. 126 was still blazing, Police Chief Conrod had encountered the harassed W/O Barbour and had asked for more Shore Patrol as things were getting out of hand. Barbour could only promise to do his best. The odds were against him, he pointed out, and there was little to do for reinforcements if they could be obtained, for the rampaging ratings had now armed themselves with pipes and wooden scantlings. Against these, bare hands were not much use.

That they were so ill equipped to deal with violence can be traced to Admiral Murray's rather off-putting naval mentality. Senior naval authorities in Ottawa had conceded that patrols should have something with which to defend themselves in addition to bare knuckles and had notified the availability of a supply of 500 hardwood truncheons. These weapons, for they could hardly be called anything else, were to be used only in an emergency and would be 'subject to local administrative authority', in the case of the NW Command, Admiral Murray, who did not come to grips with approval for their use. He was more concerned with smart belts and gaiters for the men.

Frustrated by the situation on Barrington St., the S.P. officer heard news that a fresh disaster awaited him. He set off, on the double, for the corner of Sackville and Granville where word had reached him that a liquor store was in peril. Inside the Sackville store its solitary guard, R.J. McCarthy, maintained his lonely vigil, hearing from afar the confused noises of the mob. About 11:30 p.m. his apprehension was rewarded by the approach of three civilians, one of whom carried a flagpole ripped from some patriotic storefront. When it had been poked through the window, the resulting shower of glass unnerved the trio and they fled.

McCarthy phoned Police H.Q. for assistance and in a few minutes Detective Inspector Baker and Sgt. Fry, together with constables Savary, Roe and Seymour Brown arrived, joined later by RCMP Inspectors Judge, Lloy and Kinsman. They had not long to wait till a mob of bluejackets with one khaki-clad figure came streaming towards the store, brandishing flagpoles. The glass disappeared after a shower of bricks and stones preceded an invasion. Inspector Kinsman bravely stepped outside and attempted to reason with the milling crowd. The unidentified soldier declared there was no wish to injure the police but they had been denied liquor to celebrate V-E Day and they intended to get it. Kinsman tried to explain that it was not his to give away but there was a shout of "come on boys" and in moments they were jumping through the opened window throwing flagpoles like javelins. The forces of the law grappled those they could catch and stripped them of their looted bottles. Finally, the ratings jumped over the counters and the civilians, inflamed by the thoughts of those filled shelves and stacks of unopened cartons, poured in after them. In a few minutes upwards of 500 screaming men forced their way inside to join the Donnybrook and the looting.

But the burly policemen, not hampered by inhibitive memos, somehow managed, with the help of the Mounties, to drive the intruders back onto the street. Too late to get into the fray, a Shore Patrol platoon added to the defenders. Some petty officers on the sidewalk attempted to push a rating inside but he wanted no part of the action and allowed his hat to be grabbed by the guard who offered to trade it for a door key which had been lifted. McCarthy ended up with the hat.

On hearing of this development, Chief Conrod phoned the Naval Dockyard for help. On being put through to sub-Lieut. Tunney, Officer of the Watch, he told of 'about 50 naval ratings trying to break into a liquor store', and the junior officer promised to see what he could do. Conscientiously, he called the S.P. Office but was told by a rating on duty that Lt. Cmdr. Wood had been contacted by radio in his patrol car and knew all about it. Under the circumstances, Sub-Lt. Tunney felt that he had neither responsibility nor prerogative to do anything further. Just imagine disturbing his own Captain with such a tale? Not bloody likely!

Close to midnight, still May 7th, Special Constable Jeremiah Macadam, on watch at the Hollis Street store, was filled with foreboding as a crowd of sailors and civilians began to gather outside. As well he might, for Hollis stocks were

20

1,600 cases of spirits. There were also 500 cases of wine and about 2,500 cases of beer! He, too, phoned Police H. Q. when, to his horror, he was told that aid would be sent as soon as possible but they were still involved at Sackville. Not the answer he wanted, as a club and several flagpoles cleaned out the front glass. They were followed by sailors, merchant seamen and civilians and 'very suddenly' the store was filled by 500 determined looters who ignored his feeble protests.

Presently two city detectives appeared and later a couple of R. C. M. P. Later still a patrol of five ratings and a pretty officer joined them. After that, those forces representing law and order concentrated on keeping out those rioters still on the street. A glass-cut sailor was taken to hospital but no arrests were made and gradually, as individuals staggered out with cases under their arms and well satisfied with their plunder, the commotion subsided.

As there was still considerable stock left, the gaping windows were boarded up and a token force of two Mounties, a sergeant and a squad of city police were left to hold the fort. The freeloaders had taken nearly 1,300 cases of beer and about 13,000 bottles of wine or spirits and the amount 'liberated' was enough to ensure that most of the crowd would be back teeth awash for the rest of the night. About 65 members of the Army Provost set up a barricade at the corner of Salter Street and Hollis and sealed off the now quiet area. When Wood and his second in command, Lt. MacKenzie, managed to get there, they found the road littered with empty cartons and the debris of broken boxes and cases.

From his 5th floor office window, Mr. Harold Keating, General Construction Superintendent of the Maritimes Telegraph and Telephone had a bird's eye view. About 11 o'clock that night, he had noticed a crowd form in Barrington at the Head of Salter Street. Later, he had seen a fresh concentration of rioters swarming up Hollis from Sackville and had correctly interpreted that as an imminent attack on the Liquor and Mail Order stores. Below him, all windows of the first and second floor had been shattered and about half those on the third storey. Some of the bottles had even been hurled up as far as the windows directly below him.

At one stage, he observed two trucks roll up in front disgorging, as evidenced by their arm bands, a number of Shore Patrolmen. Within a short time an unsteady line of unidentified sailors came out, loaded with cartons which they piled on the tail gates, from whence they were pulled inside by eager hands. When the loading was done, the vehicles moved off and were never seen again, at least with their intact loads and original occupants.

B. A. Redmond, Supplies Supervisor at the Atlantic Utilities Building on Salter, was also situated where he would have a good view of the unedifying spectacle. He watched five ratings in the lane behind the Capitol Theatre wrestling with a fare box which may have been ripped from old No. 126. When they had pounded it for a while against a stone post, it opened and spread a shower of tickets and silver which its attackers picked up. He could also see the rear entrance of the Hollis store where a beer chute led to a barred door. Three navy men and a civilian were battering it from the outside and, when it collapsed, it could be seen that sailors inside had been trying to pound their way out.

Directly over the adjacent Mail Order was the cable building, approached by covered stairs and guarded by a stout door. For some reason, the rioters expected there would be liquor stores there and they had kicked down the entrance of the shed. Inside, they were disgusted to find only a lot of heavy equipment, insulators, cables and ladders. There was also a quantity of 16" bolts which a navyman tossed to the crowd for ammunition. He brought out an armload of insulators and began throwing them at windows within his range. Inside, a solitary sailor dashed about upsetting boxes of type; he was joined by another who meandered aimlessly about, drunkenly bemused by the strange surroundings.

About midnight, further north, 'everything was nice and quiet' in front of the Commission's Buckingham store. Robert Redmond hoped it would stay that way but he was doomed to disappointment. Acting on anticipatory instructions, he waited by the phone until he felt bound to report that there were 'quite a few outside.'

"Does it look very bad?"

"Not yet," Redmond declared without too much conviction, for it was clear that trouble was not too far off. He learned, to his dismay, that all available help was either at Sackville or Hollis and he would be on his own. He left the phone dangling as he was submerged by a wave of sailors who surged against the wicket, tore it down, and ran aground on a shoal of empty cartons. The intruders knocked poor Redmond down two flights of steps into the basement and he was covered over by a flood of debris which came after him. By the time he had managed to claw his way to the surface, eight or nine city police and a detachment of Shore Patrol were on the premises. Making no attempt to arrest any of the looters, they contented themselves with shoving them outside. The store finally cleared, the defenders found enough lumber to board up the windows, after a fashion, and settled in to guard against any further onslaught.

When Wood and his tired men appeared, he was horrified to hear, from a sailor, that Admiral Murray had been seen on Barrington Street but it was only a rumour founded on the gold braid on the cap of Deputy Police Chief George Fox who was directing operations. Wood need not have been worried for it can only be presumed that his admiral was at home, in his residence adjacent to H. M. C. S. Stadacona, sound asleep.

While recovering from that unnerving episode, Wood heard someone in the crowd shout that the Agricola store would be next. At a good rate of knots he set off with thirty five of his men, now bone weary from their exertions. Colonel Clarke sent ten of his Provost and, as soon as he could, another thirty. A dozen city police and a like number of Shore Patrol appeared from somewhere else and the latter were instructed to round up any navy personnel they could and take them back to their ships or barracks.

The night's rioting was mainly confined to a relatively small downtown area, together with the length of Barrington Street to the Dockyards and Stadacona. In the core, the noise was almost continuous, the shouting of thousands, the shattering of glass, the chill sound of sirens, the occasional scream as blood flowed. Elsewhere, in an age before on-the-spot radio and television were thought of, the majority of citizens and servicemen were asleep and entirely unaware of the night's bacchanalia. But in the angry boil head a miasma of fumes arose from the vast quantities of beer, wine and liquor gurgling into parched throats; into stomachs, it might be added, by and large unused to such treatment. Thus to the malodour of stolen alcohol in its various forms, was added the disgusting stench of vomit.

Some sailors had carried their looted cases into historic St. Paul's Cemetery. There, amidst the weathered tombstones, over the bones of those who had perished in the duel of the Chesapeake and the Shannon, or had died from wounds brought back from the Crimea, many began to drink themselves into a stupour. Others toppled over from the curbs on which they had been sitting and fell inert into the gutters, some of which were still running from spilled or broken bottles. Throughout the long night, those who 'came to' and had enough sense to recognize their grisly surroundings, lurched to their feet and headed toward their barracks, billets or ships. Those who made it, passed unchallenged through the gates and up the gangways; and , providing they did not expose their spoils too openly, managed to smuggle them inside.

For the ubiquitous Lt. Cmdr. Wood there could have been no repose on the night of May 7-8. For Admiral Murray, the night was uneventful and, no evidence to the contrary, he slept like a log. For the good burghers of Halifax and Dartmouth there would have been no sleep at all had they known what had happened; still worse, what was yet to come.

On that particular night there were nearly 10,000 naval personnel who had not yet gone ashore. Too many of them would soon be available to add their presence to the V-E Day Celebration.

# Chapter 3
# NO PROBLEMS TILL 8:00 P. M.

The position of Lt. Cmdr. Wood in the pecking order was far from clear. He was attached to Stadacona with respect to matters in Halifax. His Commanding Officer was Captain Balfour and his immediate superior was a Commander Johnson, the Executive Officer. Within the jurisdiction of Admiral Murray, but with respect to matters outside Halifax, he was on the Admiral's staff. When his dual appointment — Shore Patrol Officer in Halifax and Shore Patrol Officer on the staff of the Commander-in-Chief —had been promulgated, the Admiral's secretary had explained it; 'You write a letter with your coat off and answer it with your coat on.'

In his capacity as S.P.O. Stadacona, he had got Commander Johnson out of bed about 2:00 a.m. reporting on activities to that time. He passed on the Police Chief's recommendation that the wet canteens be not allowed to open at their regular time. The Commander somehow got the impression that Chief Conrod would be contacting the admiral direct so he, Johnson, went back to bed. Despite his broken rest he was on parade at 0900 where a religious service was being held. When he met Captain Balfour he passed on Wood's comments, adding that Conrod would be calling the admiral, apparently unaware that the Police Chief had no such intention.

Some time after 10:00 a.m. Tuesday, unable to reach

Admiral Murray's office, Capt. Balfour spoke to the crusty Chief of Staff, Captain Miles, at H.Q. and passed Conrod's request. He also gave, as his own opinion, the advisability of closing the gangway that day, or rather leaving it closed for 1000 hours was the time when leave from ships would normally commence. Open Gangway was a hallowed Navy tradition whereby, when men had completed their duties they could 'go ashore' at their convenience, rather than to wait for a specific hour.

Admiral Murray was probably not in the best of humour on the morning of May 8th. The phones, it seemed to him, had been ringing constantly. He had been at home the entire previous evening, dealing with 'paper work' till one o'clock in the morning, such is the cross of command, and had been interrupted at that vital task several times by callers requiring his personal attention. There had been Major O.R. Crowell, heading the Entertainment Committee, asking about the part navy personnel would play in looking after the fireworks display. He had dealt with that. He had been able to straighten out some mix-up regarding the navy band which had been assigned to civilian control for the V-Day celebrations.

Admiral Murray had first learned of the night's disorders at breakfast when the *Halifax Chronicle* was brought to him. There, on pages one and sixteen, was a lurid account of the pre-V-Day bash. 'Downtown Halifax was a madhouse with the mob uncontrollable' was the theme. The account, or so it seemed to him, dealt with depredations by civilians, but as Navy men had taken some small part it was just one more wretched thing he would have to deal with. To clarify the situation, he immediately rang his Chief of Staff, who should have all the answers, Captain Miles.

Miles had perhaps not yet gotten around to his morning paper; in any event, he had no report on his desk from any of his officers. He heard later from Lt. MacKenzie but did not bother to contact Lt. Cmdr. Wood. Even when he got the gist of the admiral's testy questions, he hardly knew where to start; but he did know that he had been instructed to investigate and have a report ready by the time his own superior arrived at

H.Q. It did not occur to him that a large number of new celebrants were on the verge of heading downtown, nor that it might be a wise precaution to call in the nearly 300 executive officers available for any emergency.

Admiral Murray's direct phone to the Dockyards was strangely silent, as was another phone hooked up to Combined Ops. There was a third instrument to the Exchange and a fourth to handle any overflow of calls. That one hardly stopped ringing. A Mr. Hart called from the Green Lantern, a popular and busy Halifax eatery. All such establishments had been asked to stay open to provide food for hungry celebrants. The Restaurant Association had said that members would stay open if guaranteed police protection and Chief Conrod had been unable to specify the number of men available. It was anybody's guess what would happen when the time came.

There was another query about 'protection' from Mr. Francis J. Hiltz, Manager of Stanford's, Ltd., Hollis Street tailors. And a further unwelcome conversation with a man who would not reveal his identity but described himself as 'a friend'. It was mostly about sailors breaking windows. All these, the admiral could well have done without. He decided to escape the annoyances and go to St. Paul's Anglican Church service where he could find some peace and where the messages would be more to his liking. There he was in the company of about 1,500 worshippers in the historic old building. 'The days ahead will not be easy days', intoned the Venerable Reverend Dr. Archdeacon T. W. Savary, with more prescience than even he imagined he possessed.

At 11:00 a.m. Chief Conrod convened an emergency meeting with service police officers, at the suggestion of A.S. Mahon, Chief Liquor Commissioner. Asst. Commissioner A.N. Eames represented the RCMP despite having had only three hours sleep, what with the activity of the previous night plus his normal duties and urgent phone calls from all over Nova Scotia. The agenda was the safe-keeping of the liquor stores, already once attacked. The group met in a noisy open office of the Liquor Commission, while various employees around them continued with their regular work. Not an atmosphere, one is tempted to think, where calm and intelligent discussion would likely take place. Too true!

Halifax Constable William Edward Rafters had overheard sailors on the street that morning say they 'had got the liquor stores last night and we'll get the main warehouse to-day!' He located Maurice McIntyre, who was a Superintendent of the Liquor Commission Warehouse and gave him the warning. McIntyre, uninvited, joined the meeting but, as he was only a minor figure, little attention was paid to his information. However, he was himself so convinced of its authenticity that he went to his warehouse early in the afternoon, anticipting trouble.

Those present in an official capacity expected no problems at all during the day, though they conceded that the approach of darkness might encourage some disorder. It never occurred to them that there might be any sizeable numbers of navy at liberty and therefore had no grounds for imagining that there would be a repetition of the Hooliganism of Monday night.

Chief Conrod reminded them that, as far back as April 5th, naval authorities had informed him that there would be no great numbers to deal with on V-E-Day. Major Crowell, who had sat in on several high level conferences, quoted Admiral Murray as stating that: "The Navy has many duties to perform, V-Day or no V-Day," and that, "it was intended to march personnel to a brief drum-head service and then to march them back to duty.

Conrod pointed out that he had raised the question of naval behaviour with Lt. Cmdr. Wood that very morning, and had gained the impression that he had received assurances of good conduct. After hearing that, the meeting decided that all could rest easy during the day but, as a precaution, they would post token forces at each liquor store to go on duty at 8:00 p.m. Each group would consist of nineteen, a mixture of service and civic guardians of the peace. Conrod's understanding was that the trams would not operate in downtown Halifax that day, but, when he had noticed them running, he had been too busy to contact tram officials.

Neither the Army nor the Air Force representatives felt impelled to cast doubts on the sufficiency of these arrangements. They were aware that their services had plans to occupy the time of personnel at their respective bases. If the navy man had any reservations, he knew it was almost 'lese majeste' to question the judgement of a rear-admiral who, as it happened, was at that very moment in church serene in the conviction that everything was under control.

The meeting broke up with the participants well pleased with their deliberations and dispositions. They would be proved awfully wrong.

# Chapter 4
# A RUMOUR ABOUT OLAND'S

Meanwhile, Captain Miles was 'looking into the matter', not without difficulty as the SPO was 'tied up in a conference with civilian authorities' and could not be interrogated. However, from Lt. MacKenzie, he learned that 'there had been a certain amount of trouble in town, with some naval personnel participating, but that Shore Patrol parties had assisted other forces in guarding the liquor stores' (after the event). That report would please Capt. Miles who would deliver it, perhaps somewhat embellished, to Admiral Murray when they should meet at the victory ceremony scheduled for that afternoon.

If there had been any thought of closing the gangway, cancelling leave for the balance of the naval forces, it was thrust aside. Admiral Murray would later profess to have believed that all the ratings under his command deserved a celebration and that the thousands who had been given leave on the Monday were entitled to it on the Tuesday. 10:30 came and went and, of course, the loosed thousands went pelting downtown as fast as they could. Many of them already feeling no pain as they had been imbibing the great quantities of hard liquor which had been carried back to ships by the first waves of returning looters.

At 1:30 p.m. Admiral Murray called H. M. C. S. Stadacona, where he was told that the situation was quiet. Many of those who had been let go had returned for dinner as the restaurants in town had closed up and there was no food to be had. Mayor Butler phoned to suggest that those still at their ships should be kept there but as there was, at that particular moment, no sign of trouble, the admiral saw no reason to reverse his decision.

When he had come home from the church service there was a call to be returned to Mayor Butler who had himself been called by Chief Conrod about disturbances and naval involvement. The mayor suggested that if the admiral would go downtown and show himself this would impress the disturbers, particularly the lowly ratings. That suggestion did not at all find favour with Admiral Murray. But, while they were conversing, Warrant Officer Barbour came to the mayor's home and reported that the navy was, in fact, leading the disorder. Mayor Butler thrust the phone at him and listened to the W / O confess that there was a 'party of naval men in the vicinity of City Hall'. More, Barbour thought, than could be coped with by the Shore Patrol. There were several pregnant pauses and, after each one, he kept repeating, "No sir. It's the Navy." Not the kind of news that a junior rank would like to have to divulge.

The admiral thereupon ordered Barbour to get reinforcements from Stadacona and whatever 'other places' could provide assistance. He, himself, would phone the Captain there and instruct him to put at the disposal of the Shore Patrol sixty seven men who were already in training for that section, although they would not have the expertise of a trained and veteran patrolman. Further, he ordered Captain Balfour to remain at Stadacona, to keep his people in hand, and to be prepared to send them downtown if necessary. Well, he thought, that settled that! Once again the firm hand at the helm and the reef had been avoided. Unfortunately, he could not see his senior SPO gazing moodily out of his Stadacona Office window in J. Block at a crowd of ratings who were shouting outside and throwing stones at the canteen which had just run out of beer.

Many of them having returned the night before, unsearched, with their precious booty had been satisfied, for a time, to forego the chasers. But when the booze had been

31

drained to the last drop and there was no beer to be had they turned belligerent and a 'pretty good row' ensued, during which about 200 empty beer bottles were smashed. A session in the wet canteen normally resulted in a lot of breakage but hardly as much as that. These bluejackets were not in their normal uninhibited 'pay night' mood but were feeling very hard done by. When the supply predictably expired at noon, several hundred rushed outside to vent their wrath wherever they could. When they had finished smashing thirty nine small window panes it could be seen that such child's play would not keep them amused indefinitely. Happily, from their point of view, a real diversion appeared on the horizon, a slowly moving tram! With a great roar, the ratings went down the 'open gangway' and surged out onto Barrington Street.

Tram Car no. 151 has its own special place in the history of the Halifax riot. At about 1:05 p.m. it lurched down the northern end of Barrington with Mr. Nicholas C. Power at its antique controls. He was a brave man to be out at all at that time and at that place but, like those famous Light Brigaders at Balaclava, he too had 'received his orders'. As his tram trundled asthmatically and fearfully toward Stadacona, he quickly perceived that his way was blocked by a scrimmage of some 2,000 naval men, some still carrying rocks from the canteen affray. Turning to more interesting game, the sailors advanced on apprehensive no. 151, uprooting one of its two trolley poles from the roof. Mr. Power could see the thin line of Shore Patrol trying to protect the ancient vehicle but they were helpless. The slight delay, however, gave ten civilian passengers time to jump out, which they wisely did. Within a few minutes the beleagured no. 151 had its windows smashed, its seats broken and its lights knocked out. After the Shore Patrol had been 'swallowed up' those who could squeeze their way inside (about 150 from later estimates) did so. Others clambered up onto the roof where they clung precariously like Egyptian commuters.

Leaving the one broken trolley pole still on the ground, one or more ratings somehow got the thing going and, cleaving the crowd of animated blue figures like a juggernaut, no. 151 moved of down Barrington Street toward the downtown area.

That it did not leave behind a score of severed limbs on the street outside Stadacona is a miracle beyond explanation.

Despite its wounds, no. 151 shot off down Barrington as fast as its new masters could make it. In pursuit was former operator Power who had been ordered away from his tram by the terrorists and who had sensibly decided that 'it was no place for a man who wanted to stay healthy'. A petty officer had procured a naval car for him and he had caught up to within sight of his kidnapped tram, a hulk moving south with the incessant clanging of its bell almost unheard midst the din of its screaming occupants. At that point he saw a mob of sailors weaving all over the roadway with some of them wielding clubs. He decided that they were in 'a holiday mood' and had 'some alcohol'. Indeed they had, as we shall learn a little later. They were, by now, smashing up anything which had previously escaped notice.

Lt. Cmdr. Wood arrived with another thirty men just in time to see it pulling away. He had not observed any passengers inside it but had 'seen a great deal of glass on the street' and believed it was evidence that some windows had been broken. Putting into effect naval policy for the day, his tactful persuasion soon had the concentration of sailors breaking up and moving off quite cheerfully 'in both directions'. Some of the ratings had given him the impression that they had been drinking but they were not 'boisterous' at that time.

Despite that, Wood had a premonition of trouble; at 1:15 p.m. he phoned Capt. Balfour to report his direst misgivings. But the senior officer did not seem to be alarmed that many hundreds of his charges were rampaging in the streets of Halifax, already 'tiddly' although the sun was barely over the yard arm. Balfour did not attempt to contact the Admiral for further instructions, nor did he have any particular orders for the junior officers of his command. Nor did he really have much of a picture of what was afoot.

The demented no. 151 proceeded as far as Duke Street where cooler heads looking through its broken front windows perceived a considerable body of their natural enemies, the Shore Patrol, near City Hall. After a little experimentation with the controls, they succeeded in reversing the tram. But when they had retreated as far back at Bell's Lane, it stalled and its riders abandoned it for bigger and better sources of entertainment.

Further north, on Barrington, another tram was seized by Navymen who jammed its control lever into top speed. It rattled along, more or less out of control, till it left the rails on a curve and ploughed through a store window, burying about half its length inside. By an absolute miracle, onlookers were able to scramble from its path just in time to avoid a bloody swath being cut through their ranks.

On duty at the Dockyard (H. M. C. S. Scotian to the Navy) R. C. M. P. Constable Pitts was a special guard at the gate. A sailor, walking through the North Gate, told him that hundreds of his mates had smashed a street car and were already on their way to capture Oland's Brewery. That firm was actually situated in the North end in a block bounded by Agricola, Macara, Isleville and Sullivan Streets. As it happened, Colonel Sydney C. Oland was the principle shareholder and General Manager, and he had the same interests and responsibilities for the Keith Brewery near the edge of the harbour on Water Street. The sailors who spent most of their spare time in that area knew it as 'Oland's' and it was to *that* site they were headed.

Clearly, the taking of an entire brewery by a mob of disgruntled sailors had all the potential of a real disaster. By some accounts, Pitts lost no time in getting to a phone and talking with his superior, Cpl. MacLean, a veteran with twenty years service. By the R. C. M. P. record book, the message was passed to the City Police at 1:20 p.m. and also reached authorities at the City Hall.

Cpl. Newman MacLean would later testify that he had been on duty at the Dockyard Central Gate from 7:30 a.m. on the 8th until 1:30 a.m. on the 9th. According to him, at 1:15 p.m. a sailor came in through the Centre Gate and said that the 'crowd has gone *down* to Barrington, headed for Olands.' MacLean first advised the City Police and then called the Mountie detachment.

Sgt. Walter Whittemore of the Police Despatching

Office believed that he had received a message from Cpl. MacLean that '700 are on their way to Oland's' but no men had been sent till he concluded that it must be Keith's. Sgt. James Murray, R. C. M. P. 1 / c Halifax Detachment could do better. He was able to quote the tip verbatim; 'several thousand men are on their way to Oland's Brewery.' He, also, thought it was the one on Agricola Street.

Wood had heard something from Barbour who had already sent sixty men to Gerrish and Barrington to head off the sailors. Wood's resources consisted then of a large truck and thirty smarting men and these he sent post haste to augment Barbour's lot. The combined meagre forces reached their rendezvous and prepared to make a stand there like Horatius Cocle, the Roman hero at the bridge. The commotion could be heard approaching them from a quarter of a mile away.

Advancing south on Barrington, the howling mob broke sixty to seventy windows as it went, the tars having armed themselves with pieces of scantling and assorted sticks. Their determined but erratic progress, like some malignant comet, attracted a trail of excited citizens of all ages and both sexes. And they were seen to be joined by a goodly number of Wrens who were plied with whatever liquor was still being carried.

Heroic defiance was not enough at Gerrish and Barrington and the defenders were literally run over by the now vicious mob which paused only to deal with a grocery store on the South West corner. Those who got inside cleaned out the stock of cigarettes and threw out a few bushels of apples and mixed vegetables to the predominantly navy audience with its scattering of civilians who had been following them downtown. Looting of merchandise, other than liquor, had now been inaugurated in the Halifax Riot.

But the navy ratings wanted more than cigarettes, apples and potatoes. They got up steam again and pounded south on Barrington, brewery bound, leaving a trail of broken plate glass as they shattered windows along the route. Lt. MacKenzie and his battered group attempted to divert them west on Salter but with little success. What now could keep them from sacking Oland's Brewery?

35

# Chapter 5
# ADMIRAL MURRAY'S FOLLY

To fulfill their commitments to the scheduled V-E Day celebrations, the armed services impressed enough bodies to make respectable showings for their respective branches. The RCAF was able to lay hands on a hundred and the Army 'joed' an equal number. The volunteers will be you, you and you! The Navy, the Senior Service as it never lost an opportunity to proclaim, allegedly experienced an unusual flood of 'volunteers' for the ceremony and mustered 375 ratings and Petty Officers. They were led by Lt. Cmdr. D. N. Townshend with an unidentified officer as his assistant. To coordinate the complicated manoeuvres of the combined forces, a Lt. Cmdr. Childs was appointed as Parade Master.

It would cross the mind of Capt. Balfour of Stadacona that it might be possible to use this force which was already marching to attend the Thanksgiving Service on the Garrison Grounds. He thought they might be used to advantage on the shaky premise that they were 'men of good heart and good will who had volunteered for the ceremony.'

The worried Major Crowell was just able to contact the admiral who was on the verge of leaving for the affair and who said he would meet with Mayor Butler prior to its starting. On his arrival, the austere naval figure mounted the reviewing platform and conferred briefly with Air-Vice-Marshall A. L. Morfee, OBE, Air Officer Commanding Eastern Air Command, and Brigadier D. A. White, DSO,OBE, District

Officer Commanding Military District No. 6. The latter revealed that he had already diverted the Provost forces from the Garrison Grounds to the downtown area where he judged they would be needed most.

Mayor Butler hurried up, protesting that "rioting was under way with glass being broken", requesting urgent assistance. Admiral Muray assured him that the matter had been attended to by making available nearly seventy additional Shore Patrol and that the Army had taken similar action. The Mayor suggested that the Service be stopped immediately but the Admiral did not concur as about 20,000 were already assembled on the slopes of Citadel Hill and the ceremony was already in progress; to keep that many, at least temporarily occupied was probably his only sensible decision of the entire affair.

He had received some word about an impending break-in at Oland's, possibly from the most concerned source, Colonel Sydney C. Oland himself. The Colonel was one of those legendary figures which almost every Canadian city and town possess, a wealthy man filled with honours and positions — he was an *aide de camp* to the Governor-General — and a not low opinion of his place in the fabric of society.

The Admiral listened courteously but perhaps with divided attention to that disquieting disclosure for he had just received an erroneous message that a Provost Corps officer was being murdered on the premises of the Nova Scotia Light and Power Company in the very core of the downtown area. But at that juncture he had a brainwave which might solve all the problems. As soon as the ceremony was finished, instead of having those in uniform dismissed on the spot or marched back to their bases, he would have them parade down through this disturbance to create a diversion. It was not a question of an Earl Cardigan misunderstanding the command of Lord Lucan at Balaclava. It was an unequivocal command, or so he thought, by the senior officer that would send these men to save the day.

The junior officers in charge of the three contingents, whatever their personal opinions might have been of its sanity, had no choice but to bite the bullet. Theirs not to reason why, etc. Accordingly, headed by the Navy in its seniority and followed by the Army company, Parade Marshall Childs worried them into formation. At the tail of this doomed parade, as it deserved to be, was the junior service, the R.C.A.F.

Congratulating himself on his clever move, Admiral Murray turned from the stirring scene and conferred again with Brig. White who stated that the mayor wished to hold a meeting with the heads of the Armed Forces, the time being fixed at 4:30 p.m. Nodding agreement, he sent off an aide to make a signal to the 55,000 men of his command, wishing them "a most joyful celebration" and warning them against "misconduct and destruction". At twenty minutes to four he left for home, presumably to freshen up and perhaps to splice the mainbrace, for his nerves had been sorely tried and, he rightly assumed, would be further exacerbated.

With the smart naval bugle band in the van and led by poor Lt. Cmdr. Townshend, the column swung smartly out of the grounds and moved down Spring Garden Road. The marchers maintained a creditable eyes front but could not be prevented from taking in the mind-boggling sights within their peripheral vision. Sights which told many of them for the first time that something was amiss. What were they to make of a sailor sitting unconcernedly on a case of expensive Scotch Whiskey, before him an open case from which he plucked bottles whose tops he would knock off, swigging a gulp of their contents miraculously without lacerating himself, and tossing the nearly full bottles in random directions. Much of the beer, liquor and wine ran to the gutters where it flowed gently down the incline towards Barrington. A trickle of booze shimmered past the First Baptist Church and by the time it had reached the Court House and St. Mary's Cathedral it had become a noxious freshet.

As the diversionary parade neared tumultuous Barrington Street, its band playing appropriate martial airs, there could be seen in St. Paul's Cemetery, on the starboard side, the weathered tombstones almost obliterated by the blue uniforms festooned over them, and naval ratings swilling beer in Canada's greatest open air canteen, long before the

38

Kitchener Oktoberfest had been thought of. One naval entrepeneur, a non-drinker but sales oriented, was using a monument above some turning-over cadaver as a display counter, and was selling from his cases to any who might be without. From whence this seemingly inexhaustible supply of the cup that cheers?

## Chapter 6

# THE BATTLE OF THE BREWERY

At the South gate of Keith's Brewery, Alexander Burke the day watchman peered apprehensively at a number of bell-bottomed trouser legs he could see flapping ominously under the lower edge of the door. When it was battered down and the ratings poured into the yard "like wild animals", he scrambled over the fence to escape but later returned to his post.

Lt. MacKenzie's men, realizing that their stratagem had availed them nothing, came back to Keith's on the double and took up a defensive position on the South loading platform. They lacked the strength to cover that location and, before they knew it, a sailor squirmed in through a door opening onto the platform with his mates hard on his heels. Several hundred civilians joined in and cases were being passed out in a steady stream, some of the rioters with one under each arm. There were witnesses who would say that several of the shore patrolmen gave up resistance and handed down cartons of beer to those standing below the platform.

The crowd at this end was a seething mass, almost too dense to be penetrated by the larger number on the periphery who swarmed along to the North platform where, assisted by two or three soldiers and some civilians, they used a heavy plank as a battering ram against the stout door.

At that juncture 107 Provost men arrived along with some city police who added the piercing shrills of their whistles to the already unholy din. In the face of that small but determined force, some of the rioters fled, getting away by climbing over barbed wire on top of a picket fence mounted on a five foot stone wall. When the premises were cleared, save for those lying on the ground, the Army men pulled one of their trucks across the gate at Salter Street. They had done well to have routed the advance guard of the rioters but soon a vast crowd began to congregate outside. Lt. Col. Clarke, Provost head, making a hasty count before he left, estimated that there were between four and eight thousand around the brewery. In addition to the Navy and civilians, a number of khaki uniforms could be seen and there were even a few airmen who had hitherto held aloof from the goings on.

But it was only a question of time till the dike should be breached and it happened at an entrance on Salter Street; a couple of dozen ratings slipped past the blocking vehicle and charged the door of the North loading platform, breaking it down. The waiting multitude outside rolled through in a great surge and the defenders were overpowered by sheer weight of numbers, with looting resumed on a grand scale and no power then in Halifax to stop it. Beer was drunk inside the brewery, the yard and the street soon littered with broken bottles and empty cartons. From this one source 118,566 quart bottles were "liberated" and in short order several thousand men and women were thoroughly drunk; some laughed, some sang, some fought each other stripped to the waist. Great numbers of celebrants fanned out through the city, some staggering to already savaged Barrington Street for what pillage they could find. Hundreds hied themselves to Grafton Park, St. Paul's Cemetary and Cornwallis Square in front of the Nova Scotian Hotel where they could drink unmolested and tell the world they'd won the war. Many watched with interest as their mates cajoled or coerced the available Wrens to celebrate after the manner of victorious troops since the world began.

Under the warm bright May sun, men and women made love in public parks. Carried away perhaps by the release of pent-up emotions, one Wren stripped to the buff but became embarrassed by all the attention she got, and draped herself wtih a Union Jack which had been ripped from a flag pole.

It was past the historic **cemetery** then that the parade, headed by its Navy band, first caught a glimpse of the ruin that was Barrington Street, made more frightful by contrast to the peaceful scene on the Garrison Parade just over the hill from whence they had marched. By now the band could only be heard faintly over the crashing of plate glass windows through the length of the downtown section and the irregular roar of the rioters. As they progressed with difficulty through the glass shards on which they had to step, the men of the parade looked with mixed feelings at the open store windows through which blue jackets and civilians traversed at will, carrying away what pleased them. In front of Henry Birks & Sons, a sailor held up his arms adorned with wrist watches from wrists to elbows. They were astonished to see a goodly number of Wrens, faces flushed and squealing incoherently, "staggering about in an unladylike manner". One came out of a naval outfitter establishment with an armful of shirts which she offered to all and sundry. Another, dancing along, had a Persian lamb coat flung over her uniform.

From the sidelines, bottles of beer were passed to the hot and tired ratings in the parade, emptied and tossed away. On occasion, the middle of the street was so jammed with bodies that Townshend had to swerve his parade around the obstructions, a move he had never learned from a drill manual. During one of these unorthodox manoeuvres, a girl walked out and proffered him a bottle of gin. Mindful perhaps of the eyes of history upon him it was refused but who could deny that he didn't need a little something to sustain him.

An unsteady rating, perceiving in a store window a naked mannequin from which a woman had just stripped the gown, flung his cap away and snatched the golden wig which he put on his head. He swung the plaster head at a side window and, having demolished that, moved off down the street taking out four more. Another inebriate tried to straighten the askew curls and a drunken fight ensued. Presently, they forgot what it was about, shook hands solemnly and weaved off together. Three ratings going south were throwing looted candies to a bunch of children who were trailing them. Other urchins, some only seven or eight years old, carried boxes of candies,

42

cigarettes and bottles of beer.

Men and women, old and young alike, toted coats, shoes or bottles, the latter either from their own depredations or bought at bargain prices from sailors who were doing a thriving business. For reasons known only to themselves, if at all, there were those who hugged such incongruities as coat hangers and swatches of dress or upholstery fabrics.

A yelling bunch, seeing half a dozen sailors reclining on a bed which was part of a furniture display, tipped onto the floor those who were peacefully "sleeping it off". In Wallace Bros. Shoe Store, a rating was handing out stock, as often as not in assorted colours and sizes. Outside a middle aged Flight Lieutenant was slapping looted shoes out of the hands of some ratings. "Are you crazy?" he demanded, again and again.

Three sailors were dragging a section of iron fence which they had ripped from St. Paul's. Russell Johnson, a jeweller, tried to convince another pair that there was nothing inside his store worth taking. "What's it worth to you to keep going?" he asked. When told that $10 would do it, he was happy to get rid of them so cheaply.

While a ten year old boy struggled manfully with a sack of canned goods, a merchant seaman reclined in a red leather chair on the sidewalk, graciously offering bottles from a carton at his feet. At a large office desk dragged out onto the street, a Petty Officer was writing furiously, handling out bogus discharges. From time to time, he would pick up the receiver of a phone, ripped from who knew where, and engage in imaginary conversations of a humourous nature.

Buckley's Drug Store was in complete chaos; Kay's, Limited, once a smart clothing shop, stood stripped. People's Credit Jewellers was being looted and soon would be set on fire, spreading to D'Aillards next door. They would still be blazing four hours later. Offman's Jewellery was luckier, but still filled with debris. Many civilians had drunken women clinging to them, clutching arms full of dresses. One man resolutely shouldered a pair of skis. Seventy feet of Eaton's windows on Barrington and Granville had been boarded up but these were soon ripped away and a sailor with the leg of a mannequin stove in the first window there.

43

Major A. I. Lomas, Manager of Birks, had also boarded up his fifty five feet frontage but it had not lasted. Inside the first small holes in the window glass he found two bottles of beer, a shoe and a can of paint. Although employees were frantically scooping up the most valuable pieces and getting them into the basement safe only a token number of them could be secured in the time left. A powerful rating twisted off the bronze bars from a side window and, as the crowd poured in, within a few minutes the main floor had nothing left but trash and broken glass. When he left the shattered store, Major Lomas was accosted by a Wren who offered him some shirts from a pile she was carrying. "Here," said the girl, "they're no good to me. You take them." He did not. Standing out by reason of his uniform, a Wavy Navy officer with two gold rings on his sleeve, stood swaying with a bottle, tipped and gurgling.

Barrington was not the only scene of destruction. Ignoring Wood Bros. the mob went across the road to Barnstead's Drug Store where great quantities of patent medicine were passed out to those who could not squeeze inside. "We promised to take Halifax apart!" shouted one Navy man, "and by God we're giving her a lesson she'll never forget!" On the Hollis side of Wood Bros., Mr. G. Philip Backman was accosted by two ratings who somehow believed their mate had gone inside to escape the Shore Patrol. They threatened to knock off his head and kick his teeth in if he tried to stop them from entering. After he opened the door, the pair stalked belligerently through the deserted aisles and, having done their duty, were persuaded to move off down the street.

Norman's Restaurant was wrecked and a gang came reeling out using the pots and pans as cymbals to add to the din. Wing's Cafe, known as 'The Chinaman's' was torn apart. Further on, Fader's Drug Store was looted and set on fire, from which dense clouds of smoke shrouded the building and added to the difficulty of the firemen who took an hour to douse the flames.

At Province House, on Hollis Street, two airmen had entered, ripped down the Nova Scotian Flag and dragged it along the street, trailing a drunken Army major, another officer of unidentified rank and an officer of the Legion War Services. Others cleaned out the stationery stores of Wright's and O'Neill's, tossing out books and throwing pencils to the cheering onlookers. Someone had stolen a heavy bronze bell from John Leckie & Son, the shipfitters, and a rating had grabbed a heavy flashlight which he hurled through the plate glass windows of the Pentagon Building. In almost every vacant lot there was a drinking party going on. In one on Hollis Street, two Wrens and a dozen sailors staged an entertainment that attracted a huge throng of prurient onlookers.

Back on Barrington Street the gallant tattered parade continued grimly on its way. At the rear, as befitted its position, the R.C.A.F. contingent held steady with much prolonged marking time as unknown obstacles brought those ahead to a standstill. The N.C.O.'s in the last rank, bringing up the rear, hoped they would emerge alive. Immediately behind them was a Red Cross truck and, directly on its heels, rumbled a low stake truck filled with shouting sailors and two army men. They were all waving bottles in a manner which indicated that they had not paid for them. When drained, or sometimes when still partially full, the bottles went skimming away to crash against the curbs or near the heads of the marching airmen.

It was with intense relief that the parade ground its way through the worst of the riot and was eventually halted and dismissed as rapidly as the commands could be issued. It could be seen that the Army section had been stood down but the Navy detachment was nowhere in sight. The airmen neither knew nor cared about the whereabouts of the bluejackets for whom, by that time, they'd had a belly full.

# Chapter 7

# "GIVE ME 100 MEN WITH STICKS!"

Admiral Murray somehow believed that he had outlined the parade's route and given instructions that it was to halt at King and Brunswick streets, to wait there for Lt. Cmdr. Wood, to be used by him if deemed necessary. The complicated order, if it was given at all, lacked clarity and as Wood was not at the service he had no way of knowing that he was supposed to rendezvous with 375 marchers. What, one is entitled to ask, would he have done had he known this?

Childs, the Parade Master, when he found out what was on the admiral's mind, raced after the parade and located the Army and Air Divisions, which he ordered to be moved off and dismissed. Of the Navy, paraders that is, they had vanished! He looked for Wood but failing to find that elusive officer, went to the Police Station thinking he might call in and clarify the situation. Understandably, Wood was unaware that he was expected to do so. Eventually, Childs got back to Stadacona where no one bothered to tell him what had really happened.

Unbeknown to him, some of the ratings had 'given up' and left the parade to join the fun. Some went cut off by the crowd moving through the ranks, and others were dragged away by their friends on the sidelines. Ltd. Cmdr. Townsend was hardly in a position to make periodic head counts and kept doggedly on. When he got back to Stadacona he was perhaps not amazed to find that one hundred and fifteen of his marchers had gone A. W. O. L. No one considered it profitable to make an inquiry into this curious state of affairs. The missing were never questioned about their unauthorized absence, much less being subject to disciplinary action. In any event, there was no diminution of unlawful acts either during or after 'Murray's Folly'.

It can hardly be ignored that, with the consumption of thousands of bottles of beer, there would be relentless pressure on the bladders of those imbibing so freely. Consequently, to the alcoholic fumes of spirits and the beery miasma from bottles dropped, there would be added an even more offputting odour. Indeed, with inhibitions long since lost, the ratings relieved themselves without any pangs of outraged modesty and Barrington Street became a long latrine.

There was one thing that could be done about all this, and that was to have a meeting of senior officialdom. At 4:30 p.m. these important personages came together in Brig. White's office; he had already taken the precaution of alerting the Army base at Debert, N.S. to place a battalion on alert in case martial law should be declared. In contrast, Admiral Murray, apprised while at the ceremony, went off to his residence. There, his house steward, a Petty Officer named Boyce told him that the Navy had been playing only a minor part in the whole affair and the Admiral felt that his refusal to panic had been the proper role and he might be congratulated in not allowing himself to be stampeded into inappropriate action.

He evidently thought highly of Boyce's grasp ("he had been in the vicinity at the time") of the situation and welcomed the conjecture that only fifteen naval personnel had been involved in one of the liquor store raids and even they had been "egged on by civilians". He did not think it necessary to question too closely. And if that rather low level intelligence was not entirely accurate, his input from his senior officers was equally unrealistic. He had talked to Captain Miles over the phone but did not ask about riots and no such information was volunteered. He had also spoken to W/O Graham, a junior on what passed for the Public Relations staff and to a Lt. Cmdr.

Graham without hearing anything to change his mind.

Feeling then perhaps a bit put upon to be dragged away from his home on a matter which seemed strictly in the civilian domain, Admiral Murray had consented to go. Among those who greeted his arrival were a number of distraught aldermen clamouring for martial law and, in his words, "in a state of hysteria", quite unjustifiably so in his view. As senior officer present he naturally presided, determined to reduce the high-running emotions to a tolerable level. But, while this 'summit' meeting was taking place, events on the streets continued with such renewed vigour that they would bear recounting before the deliberations of the meeting are disclosed.

Commander R. B. Mitchell, captain of the four-stacker destroyer *Niagara*, tied up at Dartmouth Dock, was not your run-of-the-mill naval officer. From the scarcity of his peers on the streets of the agitated city, it would appear that he was one of the few and the very few who ventured out.

At 11:20 a.m. he had authorized the traditional 'splicing the main brace'. Those who partook were given 2 1/2 oz. of rum in 5 oz. of water. Forty five members of his crew had gone ashore to see the fun about 1:30 p.m. and he had crossed the harbour shortly thereafter. Taxis being as scarce as hen's teeth, he had set out on foot to Barrington and then to Buckingham, noting with growing alarm the number of broken windows. He had seen about a hundred Provost darting in and out of the dense crowd but no Shore Patrol were in sight. Pushing his way through the crush, Mitchell reached Sackville where he heard rumours of the break-in at Keith's, going down to see for himself. The situation, he saw, had got completely out of hand. He bethought himself of his sister-in-law's house at the corner of Morris and Barrington, a vulnerable location on pay nights when the sailors came up from the waterfront with their bootlegged bottles which they often discarded on the front lawn. He made for that address and used it as a base for the balance of the day, from time to time sallying out on various missions.

The first of these was to Hollis Street, carrying a large pop bottle with which to defend himself. He paused to watch the looting of the liquor store there, attacked for the second

48

time and still without protection. He noticed even youngsters of fourteen and fifteen taking part; looters who could not push their way inside turned to a small grocery store on the opposite side and ransacked it thoroughly, throwing merchandise out into the street. He had noticed some service personnel, he was to say later, but the rioters seemed to him mostly civilian.

Cmdr. Mitchell became increasingly indignant, incensed at the 'sheer lust for destruction' he was witnessing. He observed two ratings smash the windows of MacLeod Balcom, Ltd. on Morris Street and was astounded to see a lone sailor staggering along with a headless calf slung over his shoulders. What was being done about it, he wondered? Nothing so far as he could see. Very well then, he would seek out the Commander-in-Chief and offer his services in a plan which he was already beginning to work out in his head. This necessitated a brisk walk to Combined H. Q. where he soon found that he whom he sought was 'out.' He had then settled for Captain Miles, had demanded of that officer if he "knew what was going on?"

"It's not uncontrollable," Miles replied. "Give me a hundred men with arm bands and sticks and I'll stop this riot!" Mitchell declared.

But Captain Miles declined the perhaps rash offer. "The CinC's in conference," he rejoined, "with the heads of the city and the other services, and they'll settle the whole thing! Are you satisfied with that?' he demanded, already turning to his paper-laden desk. He probably never heard Commander Mitchell's retort that positive definite action was required. When Mitchell got back to Hollis Street, no doubt seething with frustration, he found a mixed crowd of perhaps fifty on the rampage and decided not to interfere. As he saw it, the sailors were more or less drunk but the civilians were nothing short of vicious. Angrily, but without much hope, he phoned Capt. Miles for reinforcements and was eventually promised a jeep, which failed to materialize. Up at Stadacona, 'positive action' was being taken. At about 2:00 p.m. possibly assuming that anyone who wanted to 'go ashore' had already done so, Captain Balfour closed the gangway.

The N.S. Liquor Commission maintained a large

warehouse across the tracks and south of the CPR hotel. It was handy to piers 20 to 40, from whence stocks could be unloaded as they arrived from overseas. It contained an almost incalculable amount of liquor, including 40,000 gallons of rum set aside for naval consumption in the wardrooms and in its splicing ceremonies. There were but two security guards on duty, but of course there had been a promise to send nineteen assorted police at the magic hour of 8:00 p.m.

Maurice McIntyre, the warehouse superintendent who had been given the chilling tip on a raid and whose apprehensions had been ignored at the morning meeting, was a worried man. He knew for a fact that the big steel 'curtain doors' had not been repaired since a freight train had ploughed into them and that there was nothing to thwart intruders but a flimsy picket fence. Although the area was generally supposed to be guarded by RCMP and the CNR Police, he himself had not been challenged by any one when he walked across the tracks to what he also knew was his place of duty.

At 4:10 p.m. he had heard pounding on the building's substantial main door, steel-covered in fact. Losing no time, he phoned the police station but got no answer. Calling the RCMP, he was promised that help would be sent. When he heard the door actually being broken down he phoned again, then went out to face forty or fifty would be looters. Among the lot was one Army private and a civilian but nobody in airforce blue. Faced with endless rows of bottle cases, the sailors began to help themselves, stuffing the quart containers down their jumpers where they slid down and smashed onto the floor.

That was too much for McIntyre to stand. "Play the game," he exhorted persuasively." You can't drink more than two or three bottles each, so why take more?"

When the looters thought about that for a while it seemed to make some kind of sense to them. Indeed several, in maudlin admiration for his nerve in standing up to them, came over and shook hands with him. Cooled down a little, they chose a few bottles or a case and picked their way out and across the tracks, singing happily. Only twelve minutes had elapsed since the door had caved in and McIntyre's nerve averted what might have been a disaster of major proportions.

When, twenty minutes later, eight Mounties rushed up, all was serene. That little band guarded a few million dollars worth of liquor till, when the top level meeting broke up at 6:00 p.m. Colonel Clarke sent an officer with 20 Provost and 180 regular troopers to complete the guard. From all the vast store, a mere 312 quart bottles of liquor were taken.

The retail outlets would not fare so lightly. From 3 o'clock on, a crowd began assembling at the Buckingham Street store where four lone Mountie constables flexed their muscles and encouraged each other like martyrs at the stake, waiting for the torch to be brought out. Here again there was a creditable exercise in human relations. By jollying and exchanging witty repartee, one of the young constables succeeded in delaying the inevitable till shortly after 5:00 p.m. Then the boards were pried from the broken windows and three ratings led a mob of about 500 into the store, which they proceeded to empty to the bare walls.

The Agricola store was similarly boarded up. There, two RCMP were on the inside and a couple of dozen Provost and Shore Patrol tried to form a protective laager? Three sailors succeeded in penetrating the cordon and in opening a rear door but were easily driven off. Then a couple of dozen pushed through it and began looting. These, too, were ejected but the frayed guardians had barely time to draw breath when the barricades covering the open windows came down and the defence was obliterated. For three quarters of an hour, while senior administrators and service chiefs discussed the situation and its possible remedies, the looting continued till there was nothing left to take.

Nor was that conference itself an altogether happy occasion. Admiral Murray, assured by his Staff Captain, that the Naval Shore Patrols had "covered themselves with glory" the night before, had little patience for the civilians who yapped at his heels from across the room. Assistant Provost-Marshall Wing Commander McCallum reported that at the conclusion of the service at the Garrison Grounds, AVM Morfee had ordered that all Airforce personnel be cleared from the streets, although they were hardly involved at all. W / C McCallum had also phoned RCAF units in Dartmouth to confine all junior personnel to barracks. In pursuance of the AVM's no-nonsense attitude, a force of officers, up to and including the exalted rank of Group Captain, was out patrolling to pick up any stragglers. Colonel Clarke was also taking positive action but the example didn't spread to the Navy.

Murphy's Law, that depressing maxim that if there is anything to go wrong it will, was not suspended during the long afternoon. While the forces of law and order most needed reinforcements, an Airforce NCO and his men sat tight in the Halifax Police Station awaiting orders which never came. And two platoons of police, sorely needed, twenty three men, went off duty for lack of instructions to the contrary. They were not recalled till nearly midnight, long after they were needed. As well, the RCMP had a reserve of twenty seven partially trained men, already, sworn in as constables, and who could have been equipped with batons. No thought had been given to calling them out.

Around 5 o'clock the RCMP Asst. Commissioner, A. N. Eames, was called by Attorney-General, J. H. McQuarrie and directed to No. 6 H. Q. where the meeting had long been in progress, though some would question the aptness of that word. He found there not only all the other senior people already mentioned but also C. L. Beazley of the Municipal Affairs Department, the mayor's Deputy, J. E. Ahearn, together with the hostile Aldermen including Burgess, Walker and the well known Bert Batson of Needle to Anchor fame.

A / C Eames suggested that a composite force be formed, to encompass all available police together with officer 'volunteers', all to be sworn in as 'special constables', as required by the Militia Act, all to be supplied with stout truncheons. It was his view that only force could now win the day and he saw such a group as being a less severe measure than bringing in armed troops as the civic authorities were demanding. It was put to the civilians that the exercise of martial law would mean using arms against men, women and children, as well as servicemen. Without challenging that interpretation, civic authorities backed off as though stung, but remained vociferous critics of the military till the end.

Admiral Murray felt that, unless called upon to do so by the Civic authorities, it would be illegal to arm servicemen and send them into close combat against civilians, but was willing to consider the suggestion. He wondered if such a group should not be headed by a municipal police officer or a Mountie but no name came forward till Eames and Crowell suggested that of Captain Robertson of the Dockyard. The admiral demurred, for that officer already had the responsibility for guarding equipment "for the continuation of the war against Japan and more important than existed in all the shops in Halifax!" Besides, although he had been awarded the George Medal for bravery, he had not been trained in police work. Moreover, there now appeared to be no forces which the Navy could contribute so the topic was dropped.

A / C Eames declared, *sotto voce,* that, given a hundred mounted police, he would quell the riot now. Mayor Butler asked him to elaborate but the whereabouts of a hundred redcoats with horses being a matter of conjecture, Eames would not be drawn further.

The City Solicitor announced that the Mayor's Chains of Office did not give him the power to read the Riot Act; that was a matter for the Attorney-General to decide. The Mayor could, however, impose a curfew and when a consensus was reached by those present he declared it. At 5:35 p.m. Mayor Butler went on the air and announced that V-E Day was officially over, with a curfew to commence at 8:00 p.m. After checking the legality of the move with the Justice Department in Ottawa, Brig. White authorized Debert to form a troop convoy at once, to enforce it.

At 6:00 o'clock, Admiral Murray suddenly remembered that he had nearly 400 men from the parade which he could use and phoned Capt. Balfour to send them out. They could assist the Shore Patrol, he thought, in the unruly South end and try to sweep up as many as they could. As we have seen, the "400 fit marchers" were about as chimerical a force as Eames 100 horsemen, the fatigued survivors resting in barracks. However, many of the Shore Patrol personnel, on their own initiative, had found sticks of one kind or another. When the SPO realized that the 'friendly persuasion policy' had gone out the window, he procured about 150 heavy axe handles from stores and distributed them. The men spat on their hands when they were informed that Admiral Murray and Mayor Butler would be taking to the streets in a sound truck and would require an armed escort to safeguard their persons.

R. J. Rankin, Managing Editor of the *Halifax Herald* had been in his office most of the afternoon and welcomed a visit from H. P. McKeen, K. C. with whom he discussed the situation outside their windows. McKeen finally decided to phone the Hon. Douglas C. Abbott, Minister of Naval Service, to ensure that the flammatory situation was known in the capital. At 4:43 p.m. the *Halifax Star* had telegraphed the three Ministers for National Defence and had received the improbable replies that their information was that the situation was "well in hand", perhaps the stock answer to cover any emergency.

A message was left for Mr. Abbott who was, ironically at that moment making a speech on Parliament Hill extolling the virtues of His Majesty's Canadian Navy. When he was able to return the call, the lawyer's wife found herself outlining the day's events, stressing the seriousness of the riot. Later, some time after 6:00 p.m. Mr. Rankin, having written off Admiral Murray as a useful contact, phoned the Hon. J. L. Ilsley, Acting Prime Minister, and put him in the picture. It was, apparently, the first he had heard of it.

After experiencing some difficulty in getting the speaker system working properly and rounding up nine trucks jammed with Shore Patrol, the convoy started out cautiously, picking its way through countless bottles and proceeding over glass-strewn streets with ratings still careening about amid the debris. As the Navy was so deeply involved, Admiral Murray was prevailed upon to take over the microphone; over which he appealed to his "lads" to return to their barracks, telling them that "The Navy by its action this day has undone the good reputation in Halifax for the last six years." He concluded with the sad admonition that; "This is not a joke!"

# Chapter 8

# DESTRUCTION IN DARTMOUTH

Across the harbour the town of Dartmouth lay, itself with a long and rich naval tradition. There, although crowds roamed the streets, celebrations had gone on in reasonable fashion and there were no disturbances on the night of May 7th. Police Chief J. J. Lawlor counted on the twelve Shore Patrol in his bailiwick and had been promised that reinforcements would be sent if required.

About 2:00 p.m. on the Tuesday he had an inking of what was going on in Halifax. As a precaution, he arranged that the ferry service could be cancelled to isolate Dartmouth from Halifax hooliganism. A few days before, the Navy had removed the one patrolman from each ferry, "lest they be thrown overboard for a lark." But, whatever happened, he could count on the nine Provost and three RCMP which had been put at his disposal.

During the course of the afternoon a number of residents returned from visiting Halifax and, although they were carrying beer on the ferry, were not stopped. Numbers of naval personnel began to congregate outside the town's lone liquor store which had been guarded by its employees since the previous Friday. Manager Warren Herman had arranged for composite protection for 7:00 p.m., a time too late it was to prove.

The store's door was eventually attacked by eight ratings and two airmen, using a creosoted railway tie. Those who pushed inside were just starting to strip the shelves when town constables and some Shore Patrol got there and ejected them. That proved, however, to be the lull before the storm as the crowd bolstered its courage and made a battering ram of two heavy ties. As the doors burst inward the mob overwhelmed the defenders and in a short time the entire stock had been looted.

Chief Lawlor, along with Councillor S. C. Pettipas and his colleague Matall, took turns trying to locate the peripatetic Lt. Cmdr. Wood. When they did get through to his office none there knew his whereabouts nor of any commissioned officer to whom they might speak. They had already attempted to phone Admiral Murray but had been told only that he was in conference. It may be inferred that Capt. Miles was taking few calls. Finally they did succeed in reaching the Attorney General who referred them to Brig. White, who, in turn passed them on to Lt. Colonel Meighan of A-23 Training Section out at Eastern Passage. They were promised help "as soon as possible". When the phoners reached Petty Officer Duggan i/c Shore Patrol, he had no knowledge of a promised sixteen reinforcements but went out to lead his own litle band against rioters who had by then broken into Boland's Warehouse.

It seems quite probable that hordes of ratings, flushed out by the Murray-Butler sound truck and its phalanx of guards, had dodged down to the waterfront and headed for new fields to conquer. When Chief Lawlor realized what the ferries were bringing he had them shut off, effectively marooning hundreds of Dartmouth citizens caught on the wrong shore. Many of them hitched rides on patrol launches and private craft but many were left stranded. Perhaps the North Ferry missed Lawlor's message for it kept on its usual route but the others headed for midstream for awhile when the rumour spread that there would be an attempt to sink them.

Despite these unusual measures the crowd had continued to grow and, inflamed by some of the 1,200 cases of beer and spirits now in circulation, went berserk in the two block downtown area on Portland Street between King and Commercial. In that short distance, fifty six plate-glass windows were shattered in thirty two stores which comprised about 60% of the business section. And at the height of the devastation the lights went out, further hampering the authorities.

Deputy Chief H. Weldon Arnold gathered up what forces were available and tried to prevent further break-ins but there was little he could do to circumvent the mob. Joseph A. McGowan, a Dep't. of Transport clerk, saw a navy officer coming down the street with a lady in tow, swinging a claw-hammer with which he broke the window of a barber shop. But, between 8:30 and 9:00, help started to come in, a hundred and twenty five soldiers from A-23, leaving Col. Meighan with the feeling that he had done his part. Flt. Lieut. Royle and Sgt. Bendall of the Air Force station along the shore brought a number of volunteers so that a pool of resources was formed from which to draw. At a hurriedly convened meeting, lasting but a few minutes, it was decided to form a composite force and send it out under the leadership of Mountie constables McNeill and Sheppard. Their task, to rout a mob of about 2,000.

Chief Lawlor knew the value of a good solid baton over the bare fists which had been obligatory in Halifax. He equipped his own men and distributed the rest of his truncheons to the RCMP and to the service police as far as they would go. By about 10:30 p.m. the worst of it was over and he could breathe easier. His force had arrested eighteen civilians, three navymen, four Army and one from the R.C.A.F. At some point, thirty men from the ship *Dundas* swelled his numbers but there was, by then, only mopping up.

About 11:00 p.m. an unidentified naval lieutenant dropped in to see how things were going and was told that the situation had been brought under control. By midnight, the "streets were pretty well cleared" and the ferry service was permitted to resume with patrols on board drawn from fifty navymen under Lieutenants Williams and L. S. Carr with the two Mounties, the airforce officer and his sergeant. Guards were posted in all parts of the ships including the engine rooms.

When the rain came, late at night, some of the celebrants lay down on the ground in their sodden clothes and passed safely through the night with some special kind of treatment from an inscrutable Providence. It was a pretty tame affair, compared to Halifax, although Dartmouth citizens would have been hard pressed to be convinced of that! In Halifax, meanwhile, the brave sound truck and its occupants continued to move with caution, trying to avoid running down civilians in cars filled with loot, less affluent ones with bicycles. A number had comandeered the carts of their children and even baby buggies were pressed into service. One could see such an assortment as mantel clocks, bolts of tailor's cloth, tinned goods and liquor. Civilians had stolen suitcases from several stores and some of these had been filled with jewellery and silverware. Above their wild shouting, every few minutes, could be heard a pained voice from the loudspeaker. "This is Admiral Murray speaking...in person...Go to your billets, your ships, your quarters and your homes...Don't stand about the sidewalks...This applies to both civilians and service personnel. This is an order. It is not a joke!" Several times, after reading his formal statement, the Admiral exhorted them with: "Better go back to your ships, boys. You don't want to get caught, do you?" He had stopped all Leave at 6:15 p.m. so those out were A.W.O.L.

The patrols were sweeping up from South to North, East of Agricola, throwing limp naval bodies into the lined up trucks. When one could hold no more another took its place. The shuttle service ferried an estimated thousand unconscious drunks to their ships, most of them being dumped off at the Stadacona North Drill-Hall. Names were either not taken or, if any records were kept, they would be concealed or destroyed.

Admiral Murray had not been all that happy with his embarrassing job as 'Town Crier'. Not for himself, personally, he would maintain; but, by exposing his senior body to possible indignities the mystique of the Commander-in-Chief was being imperilled. He gave orders for all available officers, about 120 some thought, to take to the streets as well but there was no evidence that the instruction was well received, or even obeyed. Not a few of them felt that the ratings might have "scores to settle" for there was a vast and painful distinction between commissioned officers and the lower orders. And it had not taken long for the word to get around that the corpse of a Lt. Cmdr. Smith had been found on the grounds of Dalhousie University, his skull having been fractured.

58

There were also persistent rumours circulating that an officer from Toronto had been pulled from his bed and beaten savagely on the Monday night. No statement had been issued and no one could confirm the attack but its possibility could not be disbelieved in the temper of that time. In any event, there was no great rush to support the Commander-in-Chief. He tried to relinquish the microphone to Mayor Butler but was told: "Go ahead. You're doing a good job!"

W/C Howard McCallum sent Group Captain McEwen to lead a number of R.C.A.F. officers through the streets. The few airmen they encountered "were most responsive and moved off quickly". Two sergeants from Eastern Air Command H.Q. were given arm bands and detailed to guard the Womens' Division Barracks in what had formerly been the Gorsebrook Golf Club. There they patrolled the lonely perimeter of the grounds, vaguely responsible for keeping the young ladies in and their prowling boy friends out. The comments from open windows may have blistered their hardened ears, but the abuse hurled at them was the only discomfort except for the night air and the terrain.

In addition to those carted in by the Navy trucks, about 500 managed to make the centre gate at the Dockyard under their own steam, or supported by their mates. As they approached naval property those still thinking began to discard loot along adjacent railway tracks ... shoes, civilian hats and overcoats, and such oddments as a store's empty necktie stand.

Rain had begun to fall over Halifax and their appearance could best be described as bedraggled; most with their hats at improper angles, the anathema of their superiors, It was said that there were too many coming in the gates to be counted, much less have their names taken but, by 1:30 a.m. Wednesday morning, the flood was down to a mere trickle. Any visible loot was being retrieved and those showing blood were being passed along to an overworked sick bay.

Army troopers from Debert, including a company of tough paratroopers only too anxious to encounter Navy belligerence, marched through the dark streets, their heavy boots clattering on the old cobblestones of Halifax. That sound, and the rat-a-ta-tat of hammers nailing up boards across yawning windows was almost the only noise in the sorely wounded city till daybreak. There was still some desultory looting but, in general, the V-E-Day Celebration was over. Not, many would think, a moment too soon.

# Chapter 9

# MAYOR BUTLER BLAMES THE NAVY

During the evening of May 8th, a steady procession of Army 600 wts. had growled along the narrow highway from Debert, seventy miles north. They carried 1,000 soldiers with steel-helmets, webbing and rifles. The first of them were on the streets of Halifax by 10:00 p.m. and they would remain in their clothes through the night. They would be joined by sixty Army Provost flown in from Camp Borden to the R. C. A. F. station at Eastern Passage, to be ferried across the water by an assortment of craft operated by the Marine Squadron there.

Vice-Admiral George C. Jones, Chief of Navy Staff, brought to Halifax by the illness of his father, arrived next day, at noon, by plane. He would be closeted with Rear-Admiral Murray for what can only be imagined as a stormy and reproachful tête à tête. Interviewed briefly as he waited for his T. C. A. flight back, Admiral Jones issued the following statement: "I will be in my office by 2 o'clock and I propose to direct the fullest personal attention to this situation. I have not had time to carefully survey the situation, but the disturbances are most disgraceful. So far as I am concerned the fullest and most sweeping investigation of any part the Royal Canadian Navy played in yesterday's riots will be made."

The day after the riot, Halifax was like a ghost town in the early morning light. In the pillaged plundered heart of the city, the still running gutters washed a straggle of new shoes.

61

The streets were covered with glass, littered with cartons and debris. Here a drawer-open cash register; there, three filing cabinets with contents strewed and marked by muddy footprints. Curfew still prevailed and armed soldiers clomped along the sidewalks or stood back in a shadowed shattered doorway to roll cigarettes. Soon a cleaning detail would remove the worst of the litter and, when that had been done, wide-eyed men and women would be drawn from all over to gawk at the scene of carnage. Their incredulous expressions might have matched the looks on the faces of those who first saw Buchenwald thrown open to view.

In the editorial offices of *The Chronicle, The Herald, The Star* and *The Mail,* purple prose was being fed to the presses. *The Mail* carried a large black headline RIOT LOSS MILLION; a sub-headline read 'Reign of Terror Disgrace to Whole Dominion'. 'Calamity and disaster.' It declared, "The main business community of Halifax has been wrecked and looted. While the rest of Canada was celebrating joyously over peace in Europe, the business districts of Halifax (and of Dartmouth as well) were being reduced to a shambles. Had the Germans been able to break into this area at any time during the war, they could not have done a more thorough job of looting and destruction. It was anarchy while it lasted — and it lasted a long time — for two nights and a day ... a complete breakdown in authority, in discipline ... vandalism, ugly and vicious, wholesale, unleashed and uncontrolled. Many businessmen of this City, many citizens of the City, have been ruined, not only have their places of business been wrecked, but their stocks have been looted, cleaned out."

"It will be weeks before the business life of this community returns to anything resembling normal. And how some of the victims of this reign of terror are going to resume business, is a proposition that passes understanding. Sections of 'blitzed' London could not have looked worse than did Halifax yesterday afternoon and last night. It was bad enough by the time yesterday morning arrived, but what happened yesterday afternoon, and last night represented as systematic a carnival of destruction and looting as any community on this continent has ever seen or ever will see. Not even the 'pattern bombing' of the German air force could have done it more systematically, more thoroughly. And it was all so utterly senseless, so insensate ... mob violence, mob-rule, without a semblance of law and order, without a spark of reason or justification in the whole shocking, sickening spectacle from start to finish."

The editorial went on to make the point: "While members of the three services took part in these mob scenes, this wholesale looting and destruction, the members of one service — the Navy — were most prominent. Men in naval uniform were the ring-leaders and represented the main body of the smashers and looters, joined by civilians, men and women, some mere boys. It had to be seen to be believed. And the most extraordinary spectacle of all was to see hundreds of supposedly sane human beings, in uniform and out of it, going about the streets with loads of loot ... going about without much shame, without apology, their arms full of other people's property, as though they had gone into stores and bought it, instead of realizing that they were parties to the most violent kind of robbery."

Under columnist Frank Doyle's by-line, readers learned some of the details: "Commercial Halifax from Ocean Terminals to Pier Two and beyond toward Africville, from waterfront wharves to Agricola Street's smaller shops lies in wreckage today; acres of plate glass strewn in the streets and looted store stocks are mangled and trampled on floors and pavements sticky with rain and debris, aftermath of a Victory Day riot that raged unchecked for hours and cost the City a sum ranging well into the millions. Dartmouth also was involved as the afternoon wore on and transport across the harbour was suspended as crazed men tried to set the ferries afire, smashed into business places and added rape to the list of crimes."

"Two flame-wracked hulks of buildings on Hollis and Barrington Streets are believed to be the work of incendiarists. They touched off the flames at the peak of the wild disorders which saw thousands of service men, mostly from the Navy — whatever comfort that may be to Army and Air Force — mingled with civilians in an orgy of drunken destruction. In the

63

jails are a few score of the many thousands of drunken and hysterical men and women — service and civilian alike — youths, and calculating vultures who flocked to the scene to reap what others had sowed in destruction. Police records show 64 already facing charges, 10 sailors, who were released last night because cells were overflowing, to be brought in again and 15 persons are being summoned."

"In hospitals — naval, military and civilian — are an unstated number of victims. Slashing, gashings and concussions were common as the rioters fought among themselves, tossed heavy objects from upper storeys of buildings or dived past jagged arrows of plate glass into commercial establishments. In the Morgue is the body of a sailor who drank himself to death Monday night. In barracks, aboard ships and in homes are hundreds more who were beaten or injured in the worst outbreak in the City's 186-year old experience with war and congregations of British, Canadian and foreign military and naval forces."

Below the heading 'Establish the Responsibility' it was pointed out that the "sinister threat was passed about for years that 'this town' was to be 'taken apart' when the time arrived. The time arrived. 'This town' was 'taken apart' ... And the public wants to know what precautions were taken by the responsible authorities, Service and Civil?"

It asked, echoed by the other papers, groups and individuals: "For the reign of terror that swept this community for two nights and a day during the V-E Day period, where does the responsibility lie? Could the disaster have been prevented, and what measures, if any, were taken to prevent it? The public will expect — the public demands the most searching, the most sweeping investigation by the highest authority to fix the responsibility."

"When the investigation is held and the responsibility is fixed, if it is found that any officer of any Service, no matter what his rank or station may be, has been lax in his duty or recreant in his duty, then his case should be dealt with promptly and effectively by the appropriate authorities. Grave allegations are being made in various quarters today, and directed at the naval authorities in particular, but this newspaper is prepared to await the results of the investigation and inquiry, which must be held without delay."

Riot and looting photographs appeared in nine inside pages telling more graphically than the reputed thousand words, just what it had been like. On page four was a photograph of the bemedalled Vice-Admiral Jones with his assurance that a strict Navy inquiry would be instituted. What would happen to it?

Readers were warned that the curfew which had been lifted at daybreak would be reimposed and persons "who venture into the streets without written permission from the Police Chief or the Mayor would be liable for arrest." While they could still move about, store owners wandered aghast through the shambles to find that there was more damage than had even first appeared. The water from D'Aillard's fire had rushed into the basement next door and the Woolworth stock there was largely ruined. A list of stores which would be closed indefinitely was published;

Wallace Bros.
Woolworth's
The Green Lantern
Metropolitan
Hudson's
Kline's
Henry Birks
Zellers, Ltd.
Colwell Bros.
Mitchell Fur Co.
Phinney's

One concern which was open and doing a thriving business was the Post Office. Never had been seen such an abundance of odd sized parcels appearing hastily wrapped. They had been brought in for despatch to addresses all over Canada, bearing the current purple 50¢ Munitions Factory and the $1.00 blue destroyer stamp, for the bundles were inclined to be heavy and some of them gurgled. All in vain, however, as the police descended into the sorting room and confiscated the lot for possible evidence.

After a short tour of Barrington Street, Mayor Butler fired off a telegram to Acting Prime Minister Ilsley, laying blame for the Victory riots on the Navy, and stating that Halifax expected the Government in Ottawa to compensate for the devastation. The reply would advise that "E. L. Cousins, Wartime Administrator of Canadian Atlantic Ports had been instructed to make an immediate sweeping investigation of the disorders and report his findings."

Donald Gordon, Federal Chairman of the Wartime Prices & Trade Board, announced that he would do everything to rush needed supplies to Halifax but held out little hope regarding the replacement of plate glass windows. W. C. Oxner, the local representative, added that "many stores will just have to keep their windows boarded up as the short supply won't come close to the thousands of pieces needed."

Made public was a signed statement by A. V. M. Morfee, which outlined the position of his Command: "It is indeed deplorable that such events marred the celebration on such a momentous day in the history of Canada. The enthusiasm and joy that the dark days of the past years are over can well be understood. But when we count our losses overseas and the task that lies ahead in the Pacific, it seems inconceivable that some should take advantage of vandalism practiced by the enemy we have just conquered. Fortunately, I can say for the Air Force that the hour of victory in Europe has been celebrated in the sober spirit that the occasion demands. Airmen and airwomen were encouraged to stay with their units, where entertainment was provided. I can assure the people of Halifax that the facilities of the R.C.A.F. have been and will be at the disposal of the proper authorities to maintain order among Air Force personnel."

Brigadier White appended his signature to a parallel statement: "It is regrettable that just as we were about to celebrate this memorable day, such unfortunate incidents as those which broke out in Halifax, occurred to mar the occasion!"

Following a meeting called by Mayor Butler on May 8th, attended by civil authorities and the heads of the armed services, all servicemen in the city were ordered back to quarters. The military Provost, assisted by officers and men from other units implemented the order. As well, an extra force was ordered into Halifax to stand by as a potential 'Aid to Civil Power' "if such aid should be requested by the proper civil authorities."

It may safely be assumed that the short confrontation with his superior was not among Admiral Murray's happier memories of a long and honourable career. It is not improbable that the Command passed from his hands on that occasion, although no such action was made public.

He had been advised by Petty Officer Boyce that only a handful of naval men had been involved and even they had been 'egged on' by the wretched civilians. Other informants, whose names he later had difficulty in remembering, strengthened the same comforting theory. Presently, he may have begun to believe that really *he* was the injured party, and to brood upon his misfortune. In conjunction with the Navy Public Relations unit, it proved not too difficult to maintain the conviction of innocence. From that source, an unsigned statement appeared, purporting to be from Admiral Murray. Startled Haligonians could hardly believe their eyes when they read it in the local papers that day.

"During the rioting of civilians and service personnel in Halifax on Tuesday May 8th, a number of Naval ratings became implicated. The Shore Patrols and Service Police of the three services continued as usual, at the assistance of the Civil Police and the Mayor was in consultation with the heads of three services. As a result of this consultation, arrangements were made to augment the Shore Patrols and Service Police. Immediately it was decided by his worship the Mayor to cancel festivities and order a curfew, I personally, in company with the Mayor, went around the streets of Halifax with a loudspeaker truck."

"On an appeal by the Mayor to the civil population and a direct order from myself to the service personnel, all Navy Army, and Air Force men and women returned to their barracks or billets. The restrictions placed by the Mayor upon freedom of movement of civil population is being relaxed in the daytime. That placed upon the service personnel is being retained until the heads of the three services are satisfied that no further danger of a similar incident exists.

"During the rioting, several of the liquor stores were broken into and the bootlegging trade is now in possession of considerable stocks. It is assumed that adequate measures will be taken by the civil power to control this traffic. When that has been done, I do not anticipate any further trouble. In the meantime, drunkenness of any kind among service personnel is being treated as a serious offence.

"I am satisfied that though service personnel were present during the whole of the afternoon, in almost all cases, particularly at the looting of Keith's Brewery, and the orgy of window breaking along Barrington Street, civilians led the assault and encouraged service personnel to take part. I am also satisfied that the participation of service personnel, though no doubt reprehensible, was dictated more by drunkenness and excitement than by any desire for loot, and that the major portion of such looting as did take place was perpetrated by the civil population.

"I need refer you only to the proportion of civilians to servicemen in any of the pictures shown in today's issue of the *Halifax Daily Star* and *The Halifax Mail*. Until further notice, service personnel are being confined to their barracks or ships, with the exception of those billetted in the town, who will be allowed to proceed by the shortest route to and from their place of duty. It will be realized that the maintenance of law and order is a function of the civil government. Adequate forces have been made available to enforce the law at any time the civil power decides it is necessary to call upon it."

SO! Admiral Murray was blaming civilians now, was he? And did he think "incident" was quite the right word to describe the brutal beating of Halifax? Mayor Butler took to the radio at 7:00 p.m. that evening to refute the Admiral's mind-boggling declamation and to submit one of his own:

"As Mayor of your city, I wish to acquaint you with the events which led up to the shocking 'incidents' which occurred in this city Monday night and Tuesday. At the termination of the fireworks display on Monday night it became apparent to the police force of the city that a troublesome condition was

68

arising in the downtown districts. The Chief of Police was on duty in his office and was in personal contact with the officers in charge of the patrols of the Armed Services.

Between the hours of 11 and 12 o'clock on Monday night after learning from the service patrols that the situation had gotten beyond their control and they had consequently lost confidence, the Chief of Police endeavoured to get in touch by telephone with Admiral Murray. He telephoned the Admiral's office but was unable to locate the Admiral personally, and consequently was put in touch with an officer stated to be the next in command. The Chief of Police explained the situation to him but did not receive any assurance that further assistance would be forthcoming. You are aware of the incidents of that night so I will not repeat them at this time.

According to the information available to me, I understand that on Monday, 4,000 naval personnel alone were given leave, and on Tuesday an additional 4,000 from this service were also released. This number alone would constitute a severe problem which of itself would be beyond the power of the City of Halifax Police Force of something over 80 policemen to handle, if in fact it were desirable for civilian police to attempt to control a large number of service personnel. Add to this number the large number of other services, merchant navy, and civilians and you will see the impossible situation which was created.

For a considerable period of time, prior to V-E Day, the Chief of Police and heads of the several Provost Corps had developed plans which on information then available, were considered sufficient to cope with any anticipated emergency. What actually did develop was far in excess of what those in charge of the police services could expect.

On Tuesday morning the director of Civil Defence asked the Chief of Police what additional arrangements had been made at his meeting that morning with the heads of the Provost Corps to handle the situation which the previous evening's rioting had shown was serious, and after discussing the matter with me, he telephoned the Commander-in-Chief, Admiral Murray, requesting a speedy meeting with the

Commanding Officers of the three services. A meeting was arranged and held at 2:25 p.m. just prior to the Thanksgiving Service on the Garrison Grounds at which the seriousness of the situation was stressed, and a request made that the Armed Services take necessary action to control their own personnel.

As the steps taken at that time did not seem to be adequate, and since acts of violence were continuing, a further meeting was requested which was held at 4:30 p.m. At this meeting were present the senior officers of the three services (Navy, Army and Air Force) the R. C. M. P., the Provost Corps, the Attorney General of Nova Scotia and the city officials. The situation as explained to the representatives of the city indicated the fact that it was not at that time feasible to take control out of the hands of the civil authorities, nevertheless, with all despatch, arrangements were made to assure the citizens that the fullest co-operation would be extended from the armed services to compose the situation. I am now able to inform the citizens that this co-operative effort was ultimately successful, and we believe that any further disorders can be satisfactorily controlled. An additional military force has arrived in Halifax.

At 5:35 p.m. I declared V-E day over as from 6:00 p.m. and requested all citizens to remain in their homes. The senior Naval, Military and Air Force Officers concurred in this action and ordered naval, military and air force personnel to return to barracks or billets immediately. Later it became necessary to proclaim a curfew from 8:00 p.m. and from the time of this proclamation the situation improved, and soon afterwards came under control.

This morning for several hours, a meeting with a number of leading businessmen, representing the Board of Trade, members of the City Council and the Attorney General was held, at which the existing situation was reviewed, and this afternoon a further similar meeting was held. One of my first acts this morning was to send the following telegram to the Acting Prime Minister, the Hon. J. L. Ilsley:

'In view of the circumstances surrounding the shocking events which occurred in this city Monday night and Tuesday, as Mayor of the City of Halifax I wish to advise that the citizens

70

of Halifax look to the Government of Canada to make adequate compensation to those persons who have suffered loss. Official inquiry will place the blame but sufficient knowledge is in the possession of the citizens as to the persons who are responsible for the damage and for allowing it to pass out of control. Immediate conference is advisable. Please advise when same can be held.'

ALLAN M. BUTLER

Mayor of Halifax

I wish to point out several circumstances which made the work of controlling the situation more difficult. In the first place, every attempt was made to prevent bloodshed and in this I am gratified in saying that we were successful. Secondly, the fact that the crowd which was rioting was made up of members of the three services (predominantly, however, navy) and civilians. As a result, if a civilian police officer had used force on a member of the services, it was expected likely that the other members of that service in the mob would set upon the police officer, and a more violent scene would have resulted.

Thirdly, the services were not in a position to control their own personnel, contrary to assurances which the city officers had received prior to V-E day. Moreover, many of those assigned by the services to keep order, deserted their duty and went over to the rioters. Fourthly, a clash between armed military troops and sailors was to be avoided at all costs.

These matters will give you some idea of the problem facing us yesterday. The danger is not yet past. I say to you and with the request of the Mayor of Dartmouth with all the earnestness and emphasis at my command that the greatest cooperation citizens can give to us is to stay off the streets. Curiosity seekers hamper the efforts of the law enforcement officers and encourage the wrongdoers in their illegal action. The curfew is to continue in the City of Halifax until further notice. Please co-operate and leave the streets at 8 o'clock. On behalf of the Mayor of Dartmouth, a similar curfew is in effect in the Town of Dartmouth.

Now this word is for business men whose places of business have been damaged, or whose stock has been stolen or destroyed. While no decision as to ultimate liability has been reached, I would advise that an immediate inventory of your losses be prepared. This should be done at once while the facts are fresh in your mind. Please make your inventory as exact as possible and in strict accordance with the facts. An exact, reliable inventory will be of great assistance in any negotiations for compensation, if any. Further, any person who has suffered any loss should immediately notify his insurance agent of that fact in order to protect his legal rights.

The implications of these riots are grave. In the City of Halifax came first the right of Responsible Government. To the City of Halifax has come the challenge to determine whether or not any agency of government can revolt against the government. It is all very well to speak of the vandalism of our citizens but our criminally-minded citizens can be handled by our own police. I commend the men of the army and of the air force who in the main have behaved in a manner befitting persons who wear the King's uniform. I speak the solemn protest of the citizens against the Canadian Navy. It will be long before the people of Halifax forget its great crime. The test now is 'can an agency of government under British law revolt against established authority, that is revolt against itself?' I assure the people that I will order the stamping out of riot should it appear anywhere by taking all necessary steps to quell it.

Men and women, stay in your homes and let those who have the difficult task of maintaining order and of guarding their business properties be free to act as the situation may require.

"God save the King."

Although only an insignificant percentage of those involved in depredations were actually arrested, a hundred and seventeen civilians had been incarcerated, together with thirty four Navy and two Army men for various riot offences in Halifax. One hundred and fifty more had been collared for what was loosely described as 'drunkenness'. The huge surplus of bodies over cells was transferred to the Armouries to await their appearance in Court, which would be held in that large building, the only one, in fact, with sufficient facilities.

Throughout that day, and for days to come, conscience-stricken citizens phoned police to tell of finding looted articles in their back yards. The Police station was crammed with all kinds of merchandise, the most noticeable being mis-matched shoes. There was even a small amount of liquor turned in.

In Dartmouth, the Mayor convened a meeting of prominent residents, and wide powers were placed in the hands of Magistrate N. D. Murray. Without a minute's delay, he named a Special Executive Working Committee to take whatever action was required to safeguard home, hearth and family. Those chosen to assist him were Jack West, Ralph MacKinlay, Colin Dunn, George Day, Roy W. Boland and ex-Flight Lieutenant Mitchell.

By 6:30 p.m. that night civilian patrols, beefed up by the Police from the services, had swept the town and its dragnet had pulled in any suspicious looking stragglers, particularly if they were 'under the weather'. The ferries were given armed guards, above and below decks, and their terminals on both sides of the harbour were adequately protected. Later that night, a plane from Camp Borden touched down at the R. C. A. F. Station, surprising the authorities as thirty five seasoned veterans rolled in to Dartmouth although no request for them had been made.

Magistrate Murray, having seen this group functioning so efficiently, could turn his attention to those poor wretches who would stand in the dock for retribution to be exacted. As a rule, Magistrates do not appear to be early risers; at least that seems so to those who await their pleasure in Court to which they often appear to come when they are good and ready. But, in Dartmouth, Stipendary Magistrate Murray, himself a veteran of the previous war, could hardly wait to get to the Police Court. There he would try offenses probably already fixed in his own mind as crying for the full pressure of the law.

A first group of eight men was brought before him, from all accounts without benefit or service or other counsel, in itself a possible illegality which no one saw fit to challenge. After the charges had been droned out, the majority of the prisoners pleaded guilty without being able to offer any defence. Figuratively donning Judge Jeffrey's wig, and perhaps sorry he could not wear the black cap, Magistrate Murray denounced the white-faced miscreants.

"I wish," he said, "to say publicly that I consider you to be the lowest scum of the earth to do what you did in following in the footsteps of the undisciplined Navy. Halifax and Dartmouth have been wrecked owing to negligence and lack of control by senior naval officers. There is no reason why you should follow in the footsteps apparently gone to rot through someone's incompetence."

Sentenced to two years in Dorchester Penetentiary was Morris Jennings, found in possession of stolen jewellery, the property of Hugh Green of Portland Street. The same stiff sentence was handed out to Allan Robinson, a sailor, who had pleaded guilty to breaking and entering Maurice Chisling's store, with intent to commit an indictable offence.

Sent to the County Jail for six months was George Dube, who had committed damage to the property of the People's Hardware Co. The second uniformed man to be tried was G. Lewis Gervais, a soldier; found guilty of the same offence, he was given a similar sentence. Another six month term was handed out to G. S. Marshall for damage to property owned by Marguerite Leslie. In addition, a number of others being arraigned before the court, fines were imposed for some of those pleading guilty and other hearings were adjourned. In the end, convictions were secured on 17 civilians, 2 sailors, 2 soldiers and a lone airman.

The total and severity of the sentences set a new record for dispensation of Justice in the Dartmouth Court. It was a town which took Admiral Murray's 'incident' very much to heart. Tuesday night, at the zenith of the riot, many citizens had literally barricaded their doors; they wished to ensure that, never again, would they find themselves so endangered. On the day after the riot, there were very few afoot and those, hurrying to inspect the damage to their stores, were in possession of passes. The Annual School Music Festival had been cancelled, along with other forms of entertainment which included political meetings, federal elections being just in the offing.

In Halifax there were originally several hundred cases and Special Courts were set up in the Armouries where three magistrates, including the renowed R. E. Inglis, had been assigned to handle the unprecedented judicial proceedings. Eighty four cases were docketed for May 9th, a record in Halifax Court annals. The charges ranged from drunkenness and unlawful possession of liquor to robbery, theft, creating damage, and possession of stolen goods. But, due to lack of positive identification many charged had been released and some evidence had gone missing as well. There were hints that some local residents had the slate wiped clean when, not being charged with a too heinous offence, there was a request from some local figure.

In the end, only 211 were indicted and a more curious set of statistics can rarely have been seen;

R. C. A. F.   19
Navy          34
Army          41
Civilians    117

Did these figures suggest that, after all, the ratings had been maligned? It should be noted that, for the Navy, drunkenness was not considered an offence till Admiral Murray's signal late on May 9th. Even so, it must be conceded that the Navy had come through appearing remarkably innocent. Could one believe that the events described were figments of the imagination? Fortunately, in confirmation of accurate reporting there were a great number of 'action photographs' which speak louder than words.

Appointed on May 10th to head a Royal Commission of Investigation, was Hon. Roy Lindsay Kellock, K. C. C. C. DCL. LLD, a Justice of the Supreme Court of Canada. In addition, there was a great panoply of legal luminaries, to be convened on May 17th. But before that could get under way, the Press across Canada had seized on the 'Halifax Riot' and were worrying it like a terrier with a rat.

# Chapter 10
# CHARGES AND COUNTERCHARGES

To begin with, there were thousands of parents, wives and other relatives who were concerned about 'their Johnny' and who had heard nothing from him, servicemen, as a rule, not being very conscientious correspondents. Consequently there was a great flood of inbound letters and telegrams seeking assurance that all was well. Gathered from their local newspapers, raging anarchy has overtaken that faraway Eastern port, about which they had heard little but complaint and nothing that was comforting.

When the three magistrates worked their way through the pending charges, aware of their duty to 'make an example' of the hoodlums, it could be seen that the Police, some still carrying the marks of close combat, had marked up each case to the most serious degree of offence under the criminal code — an understandable display of human nature.

Although the most severe sentences went to Naval Petty Officers — one for five years in the **penitentiary** for stealing, another for three years, and dozens with jail terms of three to six months or stiff fines, the hammer of the law somehow fell more often on the other services which had demonstrably been only marginally involved. Moreover, the two extremely punitive sentences had been awarded to residents of Regina and Saskatoon. When analysed, there was a curious preponderance of Western and Upper Canadian convictions. Or so it seemed to some.

That could have been the most innocent of coincidences, but it particularly incensed the legislatures of the prairie provinces, and provoked sharp cries of indignation and protest.

It was not long till 'Letters To The Editor' columns were overflowing with outraged calumnies dealing with the Halifax which had so badly treated 'our boys'. The Edmonton Navy Mothers' Club soon enlisted the support of Capt. J. Harper Prowse, a veteran of the fighting in Sicily and Italy with the Loyal Edmonton Regiment, and Soldiers' Member of the Alberta Legislature, "The Consensus," he said, "of Western servicemen is 'Halifax had it coming'." In his mind, he said, "the feeling of servicemen in Halifax is entirely justified. Halifax businessmen and landlords," he declared, "have been grossly unfair to servicemen by overcharging and other improper practises."

The Hon. James A. MacKinnon, Federal Minister of Trade and Commerce, and Liberal M. P. for Edmonton East, was not going to inflame the constituents of his maritime colleagues with total agreement but he did join with the club's contention that Navy men should not have been sentenced to penetentiary terms for their share in the rioting and looting.

The Canadian Legion, in Edmonton, passed a resolution declaring that, "the riots in Halifax were prompted by 'the gross overcharging of service personnel by the landlords and merchants of Halifax'. Western servicemen," they claimed, "have long complained about the lack of hospitality, even actual coolness, towards them in many Eastern centres. In Halifax," it was put forward, "this condition was aggravated by an almost universal tendency to 'gouge' at every opportunity. While it was true, "they added, "that some Halifax women opened their homes and operated clubs for their entertainment, Halifax 'hospitality' does not bear even a remote resemblance to that of the West."

Across the wide Dominion, persuasive and influential editors burned the midnight oil to depict conditions in Halifax which permitted, even guaranteed that trouble would be inevitable; and, many said, justifiable. Not unnaturally, local Halifax papers complained that the city was being subjected to a 'Dominion-Wide Campaign of Abuse!' They took particular exception to those comments which reflected on the city's traditional role as a wartime host, slanders such as, "Halifax is a city with no love or understanding of the real needs of service people," a west coast item. "Such signs as 'No dogs or sailors allowed' proves this," said the Pacific writer.

"We must remember," wrote one seething local editor "that Alfred Noyes speaks of people 'derided and belied by fools' and asks, 'Why brush one scribbler's tale away, for others to invent a new?' A pretty hopeless proceeding, let us admit. But one, at least, can say that certain newspapers and politicians in this land should be thoroughly ashamed of themselves for the things they have said and printed about what has happened in this community. Either they are abysmally ignorant of the facts, or so reckless as to spread stories that are as provocative as they are untrue."

When an unnamed Ontario paper pontificated that, "Halifax is likely to launch an intensive goodwill campaign to counteract unfavorable impressions which the city feels has been undeservedly spread throughout Canada," the condescension was almost unendurable.

Under the title, 'Abusive Nonsense' there was soon an irate rebuttal, "Some people in this country appear to believe that the Community of Halifax 'expects too much of service personnel'. And that when you stop to think about it, represents about the end of the limit!

"Halifax is an old garrison city, an old naval station, with two centuries of history, and requiring no lessons in these matters from any other part of the Dominion. Halifax has forgotten more about wars and the services than many Canadians ever will know. Fancy some little backwoods settlement in the inland of the country, some little settlement that grew up 'yesterday', presuming to teach Halifax in the ways of war and the services....It is just too fantastic to warrant a second thought.

"Halifax knows, as Kipling knew in his time, that 'single men in barracks don't grow into plaster saints.' No sensible person objects to boisterous fun and celebration among the men of the services. Certainly Halifax doesn't. Halifax has seen much of it, understands it, and enjoys it. But no sensible person in Halifax or in any other part of Canada enjoys — or condones — vandalism and criminal violence. The hospitality of Halifax is traditional. Many tens of thousands of members of the armed forces have enjoyed it during this war. And when anyone suggests that Halifax 'expects too much of service personnel' that person is merely displaying ignorance of this community and its people. Halifax knows the services; and will defend the good name of the services against all comers.

"There are those in this land who seem to have worked themselves into the belief that there is something 'different' about Halifax and its citizens. In the words of Mr. Churchill, 'What kind of a people do they think we are, anyway?' To be 'derided and belied by fools' is bad enough, but when ordinarily well edited Canadian newspapers, a thousand or thousands of miles from the scene, give space to abusive nonsense, it is difficult to say what this Dominion is coming to."

It is true that not all 'foreigners' pointed the finger of scorn at poor Halifax. The Smiths Falls (Ontario) Record-News, for example, editorialized sympathetically: "The writer is familiar with Halifax and feels sure that the guilty civilians were not true Haligonians, but people who moved to the city during the war. There has been much criticism about the attitude of the residents of Halifax towards the war-time 'visitors', which is in most cases unwarranted. We found the Haligonians most hospitable and friendly. Most of the critics are those who were ever ready to slam the city and the treatment they received, in most cases, was justified. All that the natives of Halifax desire is to have their 'visitors' act in a gentlemanly manner, or in the same way the latter would act in their home centres. While there, we noticed some citizens — not real Haligonians — also a few personnel of the armed services acting like a bunch of hoodlums, no doubt feeling that they could get away with anything in the famous seaport. They are the people who made it the more unpleasant for others who realized and appreciated the problems confronting Halifax officials and citizens who did everything possible to cope with the great influx of out-of-towners, including the armed services personnel, due to the war."

"True the accomodations were beyond the limit of the city's capacity. Restaurants, theatres, hotels were always crowded but no more so than in other cities so affected by the war, such as Ottawa for example. Our sympathy is with Halifax which has had to cope with more wartime problems than any other city in the Dominion. It is a great city with great people."

"If other Canadian papers," wrote the Haligonian Editor, "printed understanding material of that kind, instead of filling their columns with misrepresentation and abuse in a situation in which they have no direct knowledge of the facts, we would be getting along much better."

One might wish that Upper Canadians had let well enough alone on that felicitous note. One might wish that the war of words would have had an armistice at that point; but, into the volatile atmosphere the *Toronto Saturday Night Magazine* poured fresh fuel upon the fire in a feckless article by Lucy Van Gough, entitled 'Who's Really To Blame for the Halifax Riot?' Alas, there would be more, much more, to come.

It was introduced by a few words from the omniscient B. K. Sandwell, themselves enough to bring any true Haligonian's blood to the boil;

"Next to A. P.'s Edward Kennedy with his premature peace story, the real authors of the trouble at Halifax, were the restaurant employees who immediately walked out and left the servicemen with no place to eat. From taking food by force they easily progressed to taking liquor, and from liquor to more durable goods. There was nothing criminal about it; it wasn't really a riot, merely a disorderly celebration."

# Chapter 11

# THE ROYAL COMMISSION BEGINS

'MAKE THEM PAY! SQUEEZE THEM TILL THE PIPS SQUEAK!' The first step in the retributive process would be that much-beloved tool of uncertain governments, a Royal Commission to find the cause and apportion blame. Only then could damages be assessed and payments made in time to forestall bankruptcy for many firms which would not otherwise survive. Perhaps for the first time in history the workings of this esoteric politico-legal device could be seen and reported verbatim so fully. Moreover, a complete report would be published where it could be scrutinized by its readers with the hindsight of personal knowledge.

The Legislative Chamber at Province House, its public galleries full, was all bustle and excitement. The janitorial staff had left it so squeaky clean that it rivalled its original opening day. Outside, cameramen jostled for position to photograph dapper Puisne Justice Roy Lindsay Kellock, white handkerchief in his breast pocket and carrying an Aquascutum. Obligingly, he paused to confer with an official in the doorway that the dramatic scene might be recorded.

The roll of those taking part included the cream of Nova Scotia's legal profession, with imported luminaries thrown in for good measure:

Carl P. Bethune, K. C. Solicitor for the City of Halifax
C.F.H. Carson, K. C. for the Liquor Commission

John T. MacQuarrie, **K. C.** for the Citizens' Committee
Donald McInnes, **K. C.** for the Citizens' Committee
W. E. Moseley, Solicitor for the Town of Dartmouth
Hugh O'Donnell, **K. C.** for the Department of National Defence
Brigadier A. J. Orde, CBE, Advocate General for the three services
C. B. Smith, **K. C.** for the City of Halifax

As might be expected, there was a long roster of witnesses. Some wished to have their day in court and those who had rather been elsewhere were or would be subpoenaed. After the colorful opening ceremonies, the hearing got down to business with a brief statement on times of news bulletins by George Young, Maritime Manager of the CBC. Taking the stand was Asst. Commissioner A. N. Eames, the Mountie head for Nova Scotia, with testimony given under direct examination by Mr. Carson of Toronto. Eames had understood that each force was to have been responsible for the conduct of its own men. The R. C. M. P. had been unable to commit any given number due to its widespread responsibilites but would supply every available member for the Chief of Police to dispose of. This important witness gave a detailed account of his movements during the riot period but, like the testimony of others, much of the verbiage will be omitted in this account.

On the Monday evening, he had driven from his home on Coburg Road to Pier 20. Going downtown he had seen many members of the services and a lot of civilians. They were all enjoying themselves, celebrating good-naturedly, and he had not seen anyone intoxicated. "On the main street," he declared, "it might have been an ordinary night." However, at midnight as he was getting ready for bed his office called with word that Police Chief Conrod needed assistance at a Buckingham Street break-in. In fact, it was the liquor store on Sackville. Hurriedly, A / C Eames drove to Barrington and cut down a side street to Water. When he arrived, he turned over 20 of his men to Sgt. Murray of the Police.

In describing the interior of the store for Mr. Carson,

Eames said "it was littered with broken boxes and paper, the glass windows in the front being completely demolished." He had seen his own men retrieving liquor from four civilians who had given up the spirits freely. At the Hollis Street location the roadway was seething with people, servicemen and civilians.

"What branch of the service?" Mr. Carson asked.

"Predominantly Navy."

Justice Kellock asked the first of a thousand leading questions. "Were they carrying anything?"

"Boxes and bottles. Some were drinking as they went. Others were stopping to drink. Some were getting into the odd motor car. I'm not sure if they were all taxis. I felt," he continued, "they were drinking either hard liquor or beer, based on the fact that they were coming from the liquor store, it was quite possible, though," he assured Justice Kellock, "that it was neither." He thought that Navy and civilians made up about 85%, just about equally divided. The other 15% were "mostly Army men, with a very small sprinkling of R. C. A. F.," who he didn't recall seeing carrying bottles. At Buckingham Street he had seen much broken glass but the store was "strongly held" by 15 Provost Corpsmen. Outside, at least 50 Naval Shore Patrol were on guard. He, himself, stayed on duty till 3:00 a.m. Tuesday.

At 2:15 p.m. inspector Storey had called him about the large number of Navy headed downtown to Oland's but, as the City Police had already been informed, the A / C proceeded to the Garrison Ground service without qualms. When the parade had been marched off he assumed it was to barracks. If there had been any discussion regarding the situation he had been excluded from the platform.

He was asked if, at the top level meeting at M. D. No. 6, there had been any scheme for officers to procure transport and round up personnel. Not within his hearing, he replied. But there had been a lengthy discussion on how soon the provisions of a 1944 Order-In-Council providing military aid to civil forces could be brought about.

Mr. Hugh O'Donnell explained that the O-I-C was "predicated on a section of the Militia Act that provided violence must be beyond the power of civil authorities before troops could be called in." "That," he observed, "would need a requisition from the Attorney-General."

"I don't for a moment understand the purpose of the Order-In-Council," declared Justice Kellock. In any event, it developed that no requisition had been made, but those at the meeting finally decided to bring in the militia without worrying about technical points of law.

A / C Eames testified that no requests for further RCMP personnel had been received on the Tuesday afternoon and not until the evening had they been asked for. All told, he had 43 men in uniform, plus an auxiliary force of 27, about the calling out of which no thought had been given. He couldn't recall seeing officers of any force on the streets. In his opinion 300-350 men might have brought order on the first night, "provided they were prepared to go the full limit to enforce the Law." After four and a half hours, he was allowed to step down and there were those who then predicted a very long hearing indeed.

When it reopened the following morning, Mr. Bethune raised the point of the admissibility of moving pictures as evidence and Mr. Kellock replied that he saw no reason why they couldn't be used. Counsel then recalled A/C Eames and asked a number of questions with regard to Col. Oland. When did he get there? Was he conversing with the heads of the Armed Services? Did he appear to be in a disturbed condition? Justice Kellock apparently not *au fait* with Halifax society, had to ask who was this Col. Oland?

For reasons of his own, Mr. Bethune wanted to establish what class of persons the witness had seen drinking on Water Street.

"All classes," said A/C Eames, who knew a trap when he saw one. "It is difficult to tell what class a man is from outward appearance."

One of the 'touchiest' subjects was the undercurrent of feeling that servicemen were 'getting back' at Halifax for its socalled lack of warmth and allegedly taking advantage of what were delicately known as 'unwanted visitors'. Eames denied that he had ever heard words of **'discontent'** from any in the armed forces. Questioned as to whether there had even been rumours of such feelings, he sidestepped neatly by answering that he "would have to consult records and the competent authorities before making any statement, since the war is still on. Censorship comes into the picture," he reminded his mystified questioner.

Mr. Hugh O'Donnell took over the examination and there was a buzz in the old Chamber when he drew from the Mountie Chief an admission that Mayor Butler had told him "there was jealousy between the City and the R.C.M.P. and hoped it could be ignored." "That was news to him," said A / C Eames, "I am not conscious of it."

However, the answer brought Mr. Bethune to his feet with a request to re-examine the witness who had, so he said, "thrown considerable onus on the Halifax Police Force. What action would be taken?" he wanted to know, "by the R.C.M.P. if an uncontrolled riot broke out in front of its barracks?"

A/C Eames had no hesitation in replying. "My own force," he told Bethune, "would take steps to protect its own property!"

Counsel thought that such action was a "new concept" in police procedure, but Justice Kellock pointed out that the R.C.M.P. was in Nova Scotia under an agreement giving them specific duties. Changing the subject, he enquired about Eames' state of mind at the V-E ceremony. "As late as 4 o'clock," he suggested, "it must have been working on your mind, because you went downtown to follow up information on the brewery raid...You must have had an impression that trouble was brewing (pun intended?) and that is why you went down although you had no direct responsibility."

"That's quite true sir," Eames replied and, after he was finished, nine more R.C.M.P. paraded to the witness box, not all needing to be quoted.

Sub-Inspector Storey, 19 years service, had been at the April meeting when contingency plans had supposedly been made. He was unable to recall any information by heads of services as to numbers available. Nor, when V-E Day should be announced he couldn't recall whether service police heads were to report to Police H. Q. or await a summons. Nor did he recall that there had been any suggestion that trouble was anticipated, or how it would be handled if it did occur. Was there any indication of how many service personnel might be free on such a day? He didn't recall such information. Was the subject even discussed? He didn't recall.

Justice Kellock asked if there had been any plans to protect the liquor stores. No discussion, said Storey, just that they would be closed. He remembered it being disclosed that the Navy would use trucks instead of the regular Jeeps. He had got the impresson that the "Jeeps would be too light for the amount of business they might have to do."

"Not large enough to take care of people who might have to be taken into custody?"

"Yes." He could not say how the trucks were to be manned, nor did he recall the heads of the services saying how they proposed to handle those who might have to be arrested. He did not recall that the police were told some merchants were planning to board their windows. He had, he said, a written report of the meeting which could be produced. No one expressed any interest.

Mr. Carson was first to ask questions of Cpl. Newman MacLean. "Did you have any conversation with a sailor?" he led.

"Yes, about 1:15 p.m. a sailor came in through the Centre Gate and said that the Stadacona crowd were going to go to Oland's Brewery when they finished wrecking a street car. The rating had run away before he could be identified but Cpl. MacLean had passed on the remark to City Police.

"What did they say?"

"Thanks a lot."

Mr. Bethune wished to pursue a different tack, asking a number of questions to do with "murmurs against the people of Halifax. Did servicemen have anything against the people? Had he heard any reports about 'getting back at Halifax'?"

Cpl. MacLean had heard some sober predictions that there might be a "rough time" but had interpreted that as traffic problems; or so he claimed.

"Did you ever hear anyone express any gratitude for what the people of Halifax had done for servicemen?"

"I heard several speak of it."

"So it works both ways? I'm glad when you say that!"

Corporal James Drope of the R. C. A. Marine Squadron had been in Halifax May 7th and 8th with his 16 mm. movie camera and had taken 300 feet of film, starting off with boys "throwing carrots at the Orpheus Theatre." Later scenes showed "Navy boys with faces so happy at going home that he could not resist snapping them." He explained to the enquiry that he had taken pictures for his own personal enjoyment, and not with the idea of bringing blame on any of the services. There were other shots of the various exposures by celebrating Wrens in Cornwallis Park, and it was his hope to sell those portions which could be shown in a family magazine to *LIFE* or *TIME* or a similar publication with an unlimited expense budget. But Cpl. Drope had made the mistake of crowing over his prospects and the existence of the film had come to the attention of the authorities. He had been subpoenaed, had reluctantly produced three rolls of film for the Commission and had come to realize that he would not be negotiating with those eager American buyers.

Wilfred Doucette and Roy Tidman of *The Chronicle* and *Star* were also hailed into the hearing with their newspictures. Tidman handed in nine glossy prints of the riots and was asked by City Solicitor Bethune if "anyone suggested you should not make your photographs available here?" Tidman replied that, around the office there had been a suggestion that they shouldn't be used to incriminate anyone.

Scenting excitement, Mr. Bethune jumped in quickly, but when he tried to ascertain the paper's official policy, Tidman assured him that he knew nothing of the management's views. As for the photographs, they were his own personal property.

Wilfred Doucette identified twenty eight pictures, taken during May 7th and 8th. There was a view of Keith's Brewery with service guards at one door while a mob was entering another near by. One showed a woman in a fur coat unlikely to be her own and others captured men and women drinking in Grafton Park. Frozen for posterity was a view of several men carrying feather dusters, their provenance uncertain. Mr. McInnes enquired of him the reaction of celebrants to having their pictures taken in possibly

87

compromising poses. The witness recalled seven or eight servicemen looting in Melitides Confectionery on Hollis Street, throwing bottles at him. "One," he confessed "had been thrown at where I was." That remark brought laughter into the hearing. "His footwork was good," interjected Hugh O'Donnell, smiling with pleasure at his own wit.

Everyone had heard stories of disgraceful exhibitions. "Did you see any revolting scenes?" he was asked and the Courtroom held its collective breath. Not, it appeared, unless it might have been the sight of women drinking. "Well then, had he seen any 'intimate relations' among men and women." Doucette revealed that he had seen some "with their arms about each other." It was not quite what was being looked for. Describing the scene in Grafton Park, he told of civilians and servicemen of both sexes sitting around on the grass.

"Like a picnic crowd," commented Mr. O'Donnell helpfully.

"Well, they were having liquid refresments." The public gallery erupted with nervous laughter.

"Did you see any evidence of bad feelings between civilians and servicemen?"

"Not between servicemen and civilians."

"What do you mean?"

"I saw some naval men fighting amongst themselves."

Sgt. James Murray I / C the Halifax RCMP Detachment admitted to Mr. Carson that his interpretation of the Oland tip was wrong, thinking it was the North End Brewery where indeed there was a minor skirmish. Samuel Pritchard, the Assistant Brewer, had seen the gate smashed but after a slight penetration the Shore Patrol had beaten off the invader. Naval reinforcements had come in and by the time the crowd had grown to about 500 a great surge over the fence was beaten back.

"Downtown," said Sgt. Murray, "some of the sailors were staggering around drunk, festooned with loot 'like a Christmas tree.' " He was convinced that the troubles had arisen from "discontent, the wish to go home and the general slackening up."

"Is it or is it not a known fact," queried Justice Kellock

"that after a war, men who have been under discipline are apt to react and perhaps go to excess?" It seemed plain that he wanted the answer to be in the affirmative, but did not quote the authority for his proposition. It is true that those who have not been permitted to put their hands in their pockets for years are apt to do so as soon as they get out of uniform. Many would prefer not to be made to wear anything with brass buttons on it or, if that fate is inescapable, develop an inclination not to brasso them. But no known law of nature requires them to run amok.

"Yes," said Sgt. Murray.

Mountie Cpl. Frank C. Healey testified as to the Sackville Liquor store where he had seen a chair being thrown twenty feet from the ground through a back window. Constable Orval Duncan was a survivor of the Hollis Street affair. "We have nothing against you, mountie," a soldier had shouted at him through the planking. "We don't want to hurt you, but we're coming in!" He testified that, "very soon, they did. There were all classes of citizens there," he testified, "even children, but no air force."

Mountie Corporal Sim Hall was asked to consider what would have been the effect of "knocking a few heads with batons". It was his opinion that this might only have inflamed the crowd to violence. Constable Raymond F. Wellings described the Agricola door being smashed in by 20 or 25 ratings. Shore Patrolmen had run around to the back door and had chased them out but not before they had "sampled the wares".

Justice Kellock shook his head, bemused, "I wonder why you didn't arrest them?"

"We were expecting more attacks and the main idea was to protect the liquor," explained Wellings. He revealed that he had had experience in the use of tear gas in Regina, during the 1935 'Hunger March', but he could not tell Mr. McInnes if the Halifax crowd could have been subdued by that weapon. Later, Constable H. H. Gunn believed the Hollis Street rioters were "50-50 between Navy and civilians, with the odd Army man." Constable Douglas Glass saw the mob at Buckingham Street as about 60% Navy and 40% civilian and Army. He had

89

seen no airmen among the 500 who had looted the store till there was not a bottle left.

Mountie Cpl. Milburn was happy to relate that he had enjoyed a quiet time at the Liquor Commission's warehouse at the cold storage plant. Cpl. Jack Fitzsimmons had been in plain clothes in the downtown area at the height of the riot. He testified that he had seen a Naval lieutenant leading a contingent of about 30 directly into the thick of Eaton's. When the parade went by he had noticed an Army Sgt. Major order one of his marchers to dispose of a bottle of liquor. The private disconsolately deposited it gently near the curb where a Navy rating snatched it up.

# Chapter 12

# RIOT REVELATIONS

Day four of the Hearing started with speculation that it could stretch out for several more weeks. After Special Constable R. J. McCarthy described the sack of the Sackville Store, S. P. Jerry Adam, also of the Halifax Police told the story of Hollis Street. Among the crowd he had recognized merchant seaman by their badges and the fact that they were 'not natives of this city', although he conceded that it was difficult to distinguish individuals in the dark.

Robert Redmond, the Special Constable at Buckingham Street where he had been hurled into the cellar had seen neither the Shore Patrol nor the City Police make any arrests; they had been content to shove them outside, he said. As to hearing complaints, the only ones had been from young sailors who grumbled that it was 'pretty hard to be old enough to put on the uniform, but not old enough to get liquor permits.'

Thomas (Eric) Vyse, Comptroller for the Liquor Commission, had returned to the Main Office and Bonded Warehouse at 157 Granville Street after being told at Police H. Q. that 'there are no men available'. He placed the attack at 4:00 p.m. as the power had gone off stopping the electric clock. He had been at the morning meeting in an 'unofficial capacity' and had to be encouraged by Justice Kellock to 'Tell all you know, not hold anything back. Had they not discussed the prospects or the likelihood that there would be other outbreaks?'

"That's right."

"What view was taken of this?"

"The impression I got was that there might be no further trouble."

"Were any arrangements made then in the event there should be trouble?"

"None". Mr. Vyse had not been an invited participant but he had suggested to Lt. Cmdr. Wood and then Col. Clarke the use of tear gas. They had said it would be a good idea but did not follow up. At the raid it had taken three quarters of an hour from the first thuds on the door till it had been broken down. He had seen the painful sight of a 40-gallon barrel of costly Australian Brandy being broached and flowing on the floor. Two five-gallon kegs of rum had been trundled out and into a private car. After the crowd had left, he noticed two sub-lieutenants and another officer, whose rank he could not identify, because he was wearing an overcoat, carrying a bottle of beer. He had also seen two Navy commissioned officers running up the hill.

Answering questions by Mr. Bethune, Vyse said there had been "almost complete demoralization at the police station. They gave me the impression that I would get no aid." He had told the police that if the mob got into the 40% overproof rum in tremendous quantities, it would be dynamite. A couple of hours after the raid was over, they had found a drunken rating sound asleep in one of the women's washrooms.

Sgt. Arthur Fry had been involved at the Sackville Store on the Monday night. He told of waiting as the crowd built up and of seeing a "tall red-headed naval seaman coming down the hill, leading a band of rioters." He had heard him shout: 'There it is'. The police had retreated behind the counter to avoid flying glass but Inspector Kinsman had rallied them and they had moved out to confront the yelling sailors. He described how a soldier, the only Army man in the crowd, wearing an overseas campaign hat, had shouted 'Come on boys' and the rest had followed this new leader. Sgt. Fry had remained on duty till the small hours but had reported back when he had heard of trouble at Keith's where he and his men had used batons as well as fists.

"Did some drop the beer they were carrying?"

"The majority did."

"Who were carrying the beer?"

"70% of them were naval, with civilians and a very few Army and Air Force mixed in." Six van loads of Army Provost were there but he had seen neither Shore Patrol nor Airforce Police till the second raid which had lasted twenty five minutes, and which involved about a thousand attackers.

"What ended it?"

"I suppose they got what they wanted, but the brewery was still not cleaned out." He testified that the Police attitude towards the armed services had always been "To go easy with them and not to use too much force....We had trouble with the Navy all during the war....drunkenness, breaking windows and general vandalism."

"You'd better exhaust that," urged Justice Kellock. "To what extent did this vandalism occur — an odd occasion once a week, once a month, or once every six months?"

"It usually came after pay day — twice a month. Sometimes it was a few windows. Sometimes it was quite a few."

"You rather looked for that sort of condition every pay day?"

"Yes, we did."

Major A. I. Lomas of Birks testified that boards had first been put across his windows on the occasion of the Royal Visit, to prevent damage from jostling crowds. They had not got them up again till the afternoon of May 8th when small holes had been opened up in the exterior display cases. He had gone down with all his family and they had tried frantically to get the most valuable items locked up. The staff had barricaded the south door but, after one wave of rioters had been repulsed, Lomas realized that they were in an ugly mood. Surprisingly, a Petty Officer (never identified) had told him that the store could be saved. The Navy man took off his coat and appealed, in vain, to men on the street to join him in defending it, restoring Lomas' faith in human nature. The man had apologized on behalf of the Navy and battled valiantly but, in the end, had been knocked out of action by a rating wielding a captured clothes dummy.

93

When the mob poured in, like crazed people, Major Lomas dismissed his staff, fearing damage to eyes and limbs. He took his family to the safety of the Argyle Garage and returned to the scene. Broken, and left on the floor were a number of valuable sterling silver pieces with irrepairable damage. On his way to collect his family, he passed a pety officer carrying, of all things, a "load of brown shoes."

Mr. Charles R. Mehlhman, the Eaton store manager, had not minded the flags being ripped from the front. All the large windows had been boarded up but the small ones on Prince Street had been left unprotected and were out when he got there at 4:00 p.m. The store had not yet been entered, but about an hour later a blue tide of Navy swept in, no police being there to resist. Store employees had at first been able to talk small groups into moving on but soon the aisles were filled with wanderers who smashed show cases, pilfering watches, rings and costume jewellery. The more expensive items had already been put away. In answer to questions from Mr. O'Donnell he said that the servicemen were not really ringleaders but were mixed with civilians, many of them in hilarious mood.

A silver pencil with the owner's name engraved on it, Skipper Lieutenant T. J. Thompson, had been found in the litter on Birks' floor, giving rise to the rumour that commissioned officers had been in the rampage. But Lt. Cyril Childers testified that H. M. C. S. Ingonish had been in Bermuda on the riot dates with Thompson on board. Although he could not produce a receipt, his explanation was accepted that he had left the pencil in for repair several months previously.

Mr. Harold Keating of the communications centre was one of those who saw, or thought they saw, cartons being loaded into stakebody trucks with canvas tops, which he thought to belong to the Shore Patrol. When Justice Kellock asked if the witness had specified the beer going into the first or second vehicle, Keating was not going to be trapped. "I didn't say 'beer' he insisted, "just 'cartons'." The Justice allowed that, as far as he was concerned, he would make the inference that they contained beer. Robert Redmond of the telephone company was another on the same note. Both trucks had left about 2:30 in the morning but he couldn't prove they belonged to the Shore Patrol and, as he had not watched them continuously, they might have been off loaded again before departing.

Maurice McIntyre, the brave Warehouse Supervisor, told how Constable Bill Rafters, relieved for a smoke period, had asked if he could speak to the liquor official. They walked around the corner and McIntyre invited him home for a 'short chat'. It was then that he learned of the impending raid on the warehouse. He had taken the warning to the morning meeting but had been more or less ignored and was "very dubious" that the 19 allotted to each liquor location would be anywhere near sufficient. He had expressed "some disapproval", pointing out that the gate defences were in disrepair. He perhaps lacked the gumption to protest too violently to that audience but if he had been overawed by these senior officials, there is no question but that he demonstrated unusual courage in stepping into such an explosive confrontation with the rioters.

Mr. J. R. Quin, Manager of the Mail Order Store on Hollis Street had little to relate as, by the time he reached there at 3:30 a.m. the crowd had dispersed. Alexander Burke gave his account of the raid on Keith's Brewery; having been called a "dirty name" and then seeing the sailors "burst through the gate like wild animals", he had high-tailed it for the fence, fearful for his life.

"Why did you leave the place?" demanded Mr. Bethune sharply. Mr. Burke thought that was obvious. "Well, my dear man," he drawled, "I wasn't going to stay there to get hurt! I had to beat it!"

Joseph E. Tower, the Liquor Commission accountant tabled a statement of lock losses during the riot; there had been 6,987 cases of beer stolen and 1,225 cases of wine. As for the "hard stuff", noting that some items were packed in pints instead of quarts, he broke it down as follows:

| | | |
|---|---|---|
| Alcohol | 2 | cases |
| Gin | 1,087 | cases |
| Rum | 1,859 | cases |

| | | |
|---|---|---|
| Rye Whiskey | 944 | cases |
| Scotch | 942 | cases |
| Brandy | 128 | cases |
| Liquers | 56 | cases |

This all added up to 5,018 cases of spirits missing, something on the order of 54,516 Imperial Quarts! Quite a binge! Despite that already astronomical total, Mr. Bethune wanted confirmed that the 40-gallon hogshead of Australian Brandy had been included. It had. Mr. Tower told Justice Kellock that "a small quantity of the stolen liquor" had been recovered and Mr. O'Donnell asked the witness to find out if any seized by patrols had been returned or paid in lieu.

The Chairman of the Liquor Commission, A. S. Mahon, produced copies of letters sent to the service heads, telling them confidentially that he would close the stores "for a reasonable time". In his letter to Admiral Murray, he expressed appreciation for the cooperation of the Shore Patrol, "especially since it was found necessary to ration our product." At that time, each eligible person was entitled to purchase one quart per month. Admiral Murray, in refusing to close the wet canteens, described plans to set up singsongs, etc. "which should go a long way to relieve the impact of large numbers of joyful service personnel upon the city." "I hope," wrote the admiral, "that you will understand the reasoning behind this action, and will realize that it is not in opposition to your proposals, but is complementary thereto." Mr. Mahon believed him.

Mr. Mahon told Justice Kellock that the allotment of beer for the lower ranks, through their canteens, was 1.7 galls., per month; that is to say approximately 12 small bottles. Asked if, in view of the expressed desire to keep personnel on their bases, he had received any requests for additional beer quota, he said, "No, I did not receive any request." He read into the records a letter of instructions he had sent to all store managers: "....When official news breaks in your town you should lock your doors at once. All customers in the store at the time are to be served but none are to be allowed in once the doors have been locked....Remember this information is for your guidance and must not be divulged to any party. Close as soon as possible but do not aggravate the public in any way."

On May 5th, the Supervisors of Stores sent special instructions to all Halifax Managers: "The Chief Commissioner had arranged with the Chief of Police that should any of our watchmen find our premises being molested they should immediately phone the City Police. We understand that a squad will be kept in readiness to answer all calls for assistance."

When, late of the Monday night Commissioner Mahon was informed about the Sackville raid, incredibly he did not get in touch with the police, nor they with him. Next morning he had gone in early and arranged with Chief Conrod to call a meeting to see what, in light of the raids already experienced, could be done to avoid a repetition on the following night. It had eventually been decided that extra patrols should be put on.

"What do you mean by that?" asked Justice Kellock.

"No minutes were kept but if I remember right there were to be about 15 men at each store, city, army, navy, airforce and R.C.M. Police." In reply to Justice Kellock's further question, he said that they were to go on duty at 7 or 8 o'clock.

Mr. Carson questioned Mr. Mahon on the use of guards. "Who determined the number to go to each store?"

"I couldn't give that. I left it principally to the heads of the police departments."

"Was there any question as to the adequacy of that number?"

"I would judge that they thought it ample, or all they could supply."

"Was a question raised as to this?"

"No."

"Mr. McIntyre has testified that he expressed apprehension that the number would be insufficient to guard the stores and warehouse."

97

"I don't recall that."

"He was at the meeting?"

"He was in the building, but he was not at the meeting. He may have been standing at the back."

That reply aroused Justice Kellock's curiosity. "Is it a large room where the meeting took place?" he asked.

"Yes, the general office."

"A large room and he might have been there and you would not have seen him?"

"Yes, I would have seen him. He was in the building and the room."

Referring to the statement that Mr. Mahon had been in and out of the room answering telephones and had not been present at all times, Justice Kellock summed up his understanding of the testimony: "Now we have him in the building and in the room and you were out! Had there been any discussion about the number of service personnel who might be on the streets at a projected date?"

"No," Mr. Mahon replied. He then tabled the beer quotas for naval establishments as follows:

Chiefs and petty officers, Peregrine; monthly quota, 125 kegs, April purchases, 50 kegs; May purchases, 25 kegs, 10 of them on May 7th.

Men's canteen, Peregrine; same quota; April purchases 90 kegs; May purchases 40 kegs, 20 on May 3 and 20 on May 7.

Men's Canteen, Stadacona, quota 545 kegs; April purchases 355 kegs; May purchases, 114 kegs — 18 on May 1, 2, 3 and 45 on May 4, with 15 on May 7.

Navy League, Recreation, "changeable quota"; April purchases 500 dozen quarts and 20 kegs; May purchases, 300 dozen, plus 5 kegs.

Mr. C. B. Smith elicited from the witness the statement that they did not supply spirits for the ratings.

"Then, if on May 8th, or any other day, spirits were issued to ratings in barracks, they were not supplied by your Commission?"

"No, sir."

Justice Kellock saw the possible entrapment. "They

were," he said, "not supplied by your Commission for that purpose?"

"Not so far as I know." Mahon pointed out that spirits were only issued to officers' ward rooms on the understanding that they would not be available for ratings. There was a further question on the mind-boggling possibility of officers seeing to it that ratings got their spirits.

Mr. O'Donnell perhaps sensed a red herring and jumped into the proceedings. "There has been a lot of talk," he protested, "in the newspapers about the issue of spirits in the canteens, but spirits were never issued in canteens."

Mr. Smith took umbrage. "I never said nor suggested," he retorted, "that spirits were issued in the canteens. I can see no particular difference whether issued inside or outside canteens."

Justice Kellock soothed the ruffled feathers, conjecturing that Mr. Smith might be intending to prove that spirits were issued to ratings but the inuendo was not to be made till the matters had been established on a firmer footing. That was too much for Mr. O'Donnell who came to his feet in an exchange which the spectators seemed not to grasp. "There are definite regulations," he insisted, "in the Army and Navy against issuing spirits to the lower ranks!"

"All right. I heard you the first time," chided Justice Kellock, smiling. But Mr. O'Donnell was still exercised about rumours about spirits being issued and thought they were getting confused with the old naval tradition of 'splicing the main brace.'

At that juncture, Mayor Butler took the stand and the air became charged as it was expected that he 'would give Admiral Murray Hell!' in defending the good name of Halifax which was becoming an object of derision in some parts of the country. However, before he could get under way, Justice Kellock looked at the clock and ruled that it was time to adjourn till the morrow.

# Chapter 13

# MAYOR BUTLER DEFENDS HALIFAX

A surprise witness was the recall of Liquor accountant Tower who revealed that "some spirits had been returned to the Commission from various sources". In addition, he said, "a quantity was sold to the Army Officers' Mess at New Wellington Barracks, representing bottles seized from Army personnel and purchased in lieu of returning it." This included 10 bottles of wine, 81 bottles of beer and 30 bottles of spirits. It had been an *ad hoc* but legal transaction by the Commissioner. No one asked whether any action had been taken against those from who it had been removed. Neither the Navy or Airforce were involved.

Mr. Smith wondered if there had been any 'deals' with civilians and Justice Kellock commented that he was "not concerned with fairness or unfairness as between one or the other" but was ruling that the question could be asked. The answer was "No."

Mayor Butler then took the stand and stated that the control force was expected to be 200 Shore Patrol, 150 Army Provost and 75 Air Force, plus R. C. M. P. and regular police, theoretically nearly 500 trained enforcers. The total seemed eminently satisfactory, no thought being given to the likelihood that many would be employed on other duties. No one imagined that the entire number might be at all times in places where needed. As well, they neglected to take into account Murphy's Law, the application of which would inevitably work against them. City Council was also going on the mistaken premise that great effort would be made to supply entertainment which would reduce the number requiring handling.

As as been seen, the night of May 7th overtaxed the limited resources and situations took off out of control. Surprisingly, no one thought to contact their city's Mayor and his first intimation was from a colorful commentary on the radio at 8:00 a.m. next morning. Even then the papers did not greatly impress him and as he had not been notified he assumed that there was nothing to worry about. Later, from his constable driver, he got the impression that the disorders had been exaggerated by the media. Accordingly, he too, went to the church service at St. Paul's. Chief Conrod finally phoned him the unwelcome news and, about 1.45, Admiral Murray returned the Mayor's phone call. Pointing out that the Navy was involved and that the situation was 'very serious', he demanded that 'the disturbances should be nipped in the bud.' When asked for suggestions, he had a ready answer. "Your presence there, Admiral Murray, would have a profound effect on the rioters," he urged, "particularly the ratings!"

"What was the admiral's response to your suggestion?"

"He was not impressed by it ... He said to the affect that he did not think he could do that. As we were conversing, into my house came a member of the Shore Patrol."

"Do you know his name?"

"I do, sir."

"What is it?"

"For personal reasons involving myself in a way, that punitive action ..."

"It was Warrant Officer Barber, was it not?" asked Mr. O'Donnell. "What is the matter? You do not need to be afraid."

On Mr. Smith's objection the word 'afraid' was with-, drawn and Mayor Butler resumed his testimony in which he described the Warrant Officer repeating, "No, sir. It's the Navy." The Mayor had some reason to suspect that the W / O would not go down in the admiral's books as one of his best regarded.

In any event, it was the start of a worrisome day for His Worship. At the drumhead service he had again stressed the seriousness of the situation to a distant admiral. He had left the ceremony to see for himself what was happening and was so shocked that he hurried back and accosted the aloof and disinterested senior officer. "Did you suggest any course you might take?"

"I told him that unless he acted, I would use all the powers vested in me to get military help with the reading of the Riot Act and martial law if within my powers."

The Admiral had conferred briefly with the other heads and had returned to advise that he had ordered those servicemen still on the grounds to be paraded downtown to abate the disorders. To that, Mayor Butler made no reply as he "became aware and was aware that was all the Admiral intended to do." For his part, he went to his office and hurriedly convened the Safety Committee where the City Solicitor informed him that there was no provision in law to deal with the riot as he had proposed.

Justice Kellock wanted the situation clarified. "Am I to understand?" he asked, "that at this stage (4:00 p.m.) nothing had been done except this proposed parade downtown and that the situation was out of hand of city police and of any service police available at the time?"

"Yes."

Mayor Butler met the bumbling but autocratic Liquor Commissioner, Mr. Mahon, at City Hall and laid on him much of the responsibility for not isolating liquor stocks under his control, criticism which evoked a strong protest.

"What did you have in mind?"

"I had in mind that in Halifax there was a great deal of discontent, bureaucratic control as to the administration of the liquor laws of Nova Scotia. I had in mind ..."

What it was we will never know, for Justice Kellock closed that avenue. "Perhaps I had better not ask that," he said. "I thought you had something else in mind. At any time prior to May 7th and since you took office, had you yourself discussed what steps might be taken to isolate liquor stocks?"

"No." Moving on the afternoon emergency meeting,

the Mayor's civil delegation was hot for speeding imposition of martial law. They were "soon informed by the non-civilian crowd" that such a course was not feasible due to the danger to men, women and children. There had been some discussion about forming a composite unit but nothing had come of it. He had been heartened to hear A / C Eames tell Brig. White that "given 200 mounted police, I would quell the riot now". The mayor wanted to hear the idea developed but the senior figures "went their separate ways and would not talk to me further about it ... I asked Comm. Eames what he meant and he refused to say. The 200 could have been brought in, I dare say," the Mayor concluded, drawing a sharp rebuke from Justice Kellock. "Confine yourself to saying what you know. There is no need of saying that unless you knew where they were," said the Justice curtly.

Mayor Butler stated that he knew there had been a decision to bring in a well-trained regiment, but had not been present at that time. "I don't know where the important people were," he complained, referring to a small select group, "I wasn't invited." When laughter had broken out at the remark, Justice Kellock warned the crowd in the galleries that the hearing was not an entertainment. "Unless there is quiet and dignity," he scolded, "I will order the galleries cleared."

"You were quite satisfied to leave this matter to others at the meeting?"

"I didn't know about the meeting."

"What did you put forward?"

"I wasn't putting any particular suggestion forward, but I had gone to the meeting looking for a large and substantial force. I did not believe that small bodies of men would suffice." He deemed the consensus there was that to declare martial law would be to have the Army shooting at the Navy, which "would produce a result of terrible consequences."

"There was no thought in your mind that the mere presence of a large force would be of assistance, apart from the use of arms?"

"I felt that the presence of a large force would be effective only if it were properly trained and adequate."

"Did you have in mind that the employment of such a force would immediately mean the employment of fire arms?"

"Might not immediately, or inevitably. I had thought of the use of a body of troops to put down the disturbances."

"Did you mention that to the meeting?"

"Not of my own volition — not that I can remember."

"Why didn't you say to the meeting that that was the only thing to care for the situation?"

"I can't say why I didn't say it to the meeting...It was a very hurried afternoon."

"I'm sure it was," Justice Kellock agreed. "But if that was in your mind, it only seems strange that you did not mention it."

The Mayor testified that he had not read the Riot Act as that might have led to bloodshed and thus to declaring Martial Law, which could not be enforced. "Had it not been for the city," he pointed out, "no meeting would have been held at all." They had at least found out what was going on and who was responsible for it. As for speaking his mind, he had been much disturbed in mind and there was great confusion, an understatement, to say the least.

To the mayor's chagrin, Mr. Smith returned to the reluctance to disclose the name of the Warrant Officer. "What was your objection?"

Here Justice Kellock intervened. "Do you think I would be interested in that?" he enquired.

"I think so," said Mr. Smith, "to get the general picture."

"I had reasons to be apprehensive," Mayor Butler admitted, "of the Warrant Officer's promotional future in the Navy because certain punitive action had been directed against me by the Navy since I made my first radio speech."

Oddly enough, no one seemingly wished to learn anything about the 'punitive action' nor were they interested in hearing Barbour's testimony, so the matter was not pursued. Instead, Mr. O'Donnell attacked the civic authorities for not informing the services about changes of dates of the fireworks and street dances, and Mayor Butler had to admit that he had been remiss. "Did you know," Mr. O'Donnell snapped, "that Navy personnel were kept at work because they were waiting for official word from you?"

"I didn't know," the mayor conceded. It seemed like a picayune point. But there followed a sharp exchange between Mr. O'Donnell (who tried to manouvre the mayor into agreeing that maintenance of law and order was a civic responsibility, by implication not that of the services) and Mr. Smith who pointed out that there were differences of opinion in the legal field and the mayor was just a layman. Mr. O'Donnell defended his line of questioning as "designed to get at the state of the mayor's mind", but Mr. Smith was having none of that. "I suggest my learned friend," he snapped, "was more interested in putting words in his mouth than getting at his state of mind." Justice Kellock advised the Defence lawyer to proceed more slowly with questions to permit the witness to better answer. "I could follow them better, too," he added pointedly.

"Did it occur to you at any time that morning to check with Mr. Mahon with respect to protection of the liquor stores?"

"No, it did not occur to me."

"After you read of the raids?"

"No, I didn't look for any further rioting or trouble."

"Did you suggest earlier that liquor should be isolated?"

"No, but my predecessor in office (Mayor Lloyd) came to me after the riots and told me that he had done so."

"You and Admiral Murray agreed that rather than cancel the ceremony it would be more advisable to proceed?"

"I don't remember that."

"This is one point where your memory is blurred," Mr. O'Donnell suggested, scornfully, getting an objection again from Mr. Smith, whereupon Justice Kellock decided to clarify the evidence. "Let's get at the facts," he said. "Did you discuss with him the suggestion that the ceremony be cancelled?"

"No, I don't remember that."

"Do you deny it?" Mr. O'Donnell demanding, taking over.

"No."

"Did you agree that the service would proceed?"

"I remember him saying that they would go on with the service."

"And make it as short a possible, and then parade the Navy through the streets?"

"No."

"Do you deny it?"

"No."

"Did the admiral explain to you that the Navy people were on holiday, as was everyone else, and they might not be available?"

"To put down the riot? He might have. No one ever gave me any information on that."

"Do you deny it?"

"No."

"Did you see any break ranks?"

"No."

"What personal information did you have on that?"

"None. The statement was prepared by my experts at City Hall."

"Did you know of the work of theShore Patrol at Keith's, Oland's, Hollis Street and elsewhere?"

"I had no knowledge of this. It was prepared by my experts and I rely on it as being true."

"Whom do you rely on?"

"The City Solicitor prepared the greater part of it."

"That's the expert you had in mind when you mentioned experts?"

"Yes."

"You didn't do anything at all till 1:30 o'clock?" asked Justice Kellock. It appeared that the witness had not.

Mr. McInnes requested that the Minutes of the afternoon meeting be produced to clean up hazy recollections, sparking a wrangle amongst various counsel till the Justice admonished them. Mayor Butler then found that his memory had been somewhat refreshed, and it was shown that he had asked Admiral Murray to recall all service personnel to barracks; but the Admiral had been adamant, as to do so in his view would penalize the many who were already in the streets and behaving themselves. When Mayor Allan Butler was permitted to stand down, he may have had the feeling that somehow he had been made to seem more responsible for the unhappy events than he thought reasonable. Perhaps he hoped that the questioners would be even more on their mettle when the real culprit was brought before them.

Major O. R. Crowell, Entertainment Chairman emphasized that Admiral Murray had told him that V-E Day was just another day and that Navy personnel would be marched to a service and back again. His Committee had been concerned about keeping the restaurants open, even if only coffee and sandwiches could be provided. In the event, some had stayed open and others had closed. Somehow, he had understod that there would be only 'skeleton stocks' in the liquor stores. He had actually brought up the point with Mr. Mahon but had been told 'not to worry', that adequate arrangements had been made for its safekeeping. Later, he had narrowly escaped being run down by a police cruiser which had failed to negotiate a turn and had crashed into a building at Bedford Row in its efforts of 'safekeeping'.

In all testimony till then the more genteel word 'intoxicated' had been favoured but, for the first time the common 'drunk' crept in, and a definition was even attempted:

"Did you see much in the way of intoxication?" (Mr. Carson)

"In a state of New Year's inebriation — yes."

"Did you see many drunks?"

"Not complete drunks."

"I don't ask about complete drunks — just drunks?"

"No. Many showing signs."

"What does complete drunk mean?"

"Staggering, having difficulty getting around."

"And you saw some cold sober people?" (Mr. O'Donnell)

"I think there were some." He went on to describe his attempts to put on another fireworks display but was told that the Navy fireboat was not available. There had been a rumour that H.M.C.S. Peregrine was to be burned that night and Mr. Coxon of the Naval Fire Service wanted all his men on duty.

Judson A. Conrod, 12 years as Police Chief and 34 years on the force, said he had 86 men for street duty. He had advised Mr. Mahon that there were not enough to guard each location but there would be patrols in the vicinity. He reminisced about Armistice Day, 1918, when there had been no disorders in an exuberant crowd. Only shouting, singing, waving flags, setting off fire-crackers and throwing talcum powder. It had been two years after prohibition then but there was plenty of liquor, even easier to get that at the present time. He did not need to remind the hearing that many Nova Scotians were in the trade and being a 'rum-runner' was no great social stigma, some commissioned officers having been well known operators. In the Eastern Air Command Marine Squadron, a number of ex-R. C. M. P. Preventative Service were still serving on the Detector and the Arresteur which were on loan. They had exchanged shots with other skippers in peacetime, but bad feelings had been put aside in '39. Or so it was said.

The Chief had been led to believe that the Shore Patrol would supply 200 men for his deployment, 50 of them to be based at the Police Station. He had expected that the Army and Air Force would give him about 75 each. His own men had been instructed to be 'courteous and obliging' and not to go out of their way to provoke incidents. He had been given to understand that there would be fewer Navy on the streets than on a normal day when his men customarily had to deal with smashed windows, etc. almost as a routine. The Navy, he believed, would mostly be in their barracks with dinner, refreshments and unspecfied entertainments.

On the stand for his second day, the Chief denied any knowledge of 'secret' naval orders which intimated that the arrest of a rating might provoke a serious riot, and that the 'Shore Patrol were to look the other way'. If the Navy wished to fight amongst themselves, his men would exercise judgement. If they had to make arrests the service involved would be a party to it. He did not think it was official policy for the police of one service to arrest the personnel of another.

On the first night of the outbreaks, when he had seen that he was too thin on the ground, he had tried to reach Admiral Murray to request the 150 Shore Patrol he had thought were in reserve. Failing in that, he had finally got through to the 'Officer of the Watch' but the expected assistance failed to materialize and he heard nothing further from the Navy. No officer who brought 'problems' to the Admiral was likely to be looked on with favour and the young sub-lieutenant naturally avoided going over the head of a senior officer, in this case Lt. Cmdr. Wood.

When serious rioting broke out on the Tuesday, the Chief had only 40 on duty downtown, with about 20 on the Garrison Grounds. Even more then could he have used prompt support but he described the considerable delay in the authorities reaching a decision to reinforce him. He was still lamenting that situation when Justice Kellock recessed the Commission to June 6th.

## Chapter 14

# TORONTO'S SATURDAY NIGHT
# BLAMES HALIFAX

During adjournment, far from it being a period when frayed Haligonian nerves might know balm, the invidious article in *Toronto's Saturday Night* was sending shock waves from Pier 20 to the North West Arm; indeed from Louisburg to Fort Kent! According to the by-line, Van Gogh got the credit for the offending material but there were those who believed that this was a pseudonym for the Editor himself, B. K. Sandwell.

"The real autnor of the Halifax riot, so the old Haligonian told me, was Edgar Kennedy of the Associated Press, with his premature peace story, but it is improbable that the store-keepers will ever get anything out of the A. P. to recoup their damages. And anyhow, even if Mr. Kennedy hadn't broken the peace story at an inopportune time somebody else might have with just the same result.

"Next to Kennedy the people to blame for the Halifax riot, said the old Haligonian, were the restaurant employees. The restaurant business is an essential public service, as much as the railway and the street car business and the milk deliveries, and there is a heavy moral obligation on everybody concerned to keep them going when it is needed. Not withstanding that, the workers in all the restaurants walked out an hour after the VE announcement without notice and without authorization. If the proprietors of the restaurants had turned them out, for their own reasons, they would have howled to high heaven that it was an inconceivable outrage on the public and on the restaurant workers both. But they themselves walked out, just because they felt like it, and left both the proprietors and the public to go to the devil. The voluntary-worker canteens, to their eternal credit, continued to function, but they were desperately over-crowded all day.

"And that was what started the riot. Halifax was crammed with servicemen on short leave who had no home kitchen to go to and who wanted food. (Exactly the same situation existed in Toronto and scoresof other Canadian cities where people visit and it was only by jolly good luck and the fact that people were feeling exceptionally tolerant that there were no riots in other places. Of course service men when gathered together and hungry in large numbers, are quite a bit more likely to assert what they feel to be their right than ordinary citizens.)

"Of course it wasn't a riot really. Everybody was in a good temper, and when people are in a good temper it isn't a riot, it is merely a disorderly celebration. All the same it was dangerous, and exceedingly expensive. But it all arose out of the fact that Halifax was full of men who had been doing their bit in the war, who had helped finish off the war, and who had thought they were entitled to have a day's celebration, complete with food, when it was announced that the war was finished. When they found they couldn't buy food it occurred to them that they might as well take it, and they began to do so. But the next idea was that if they were going to take things they might as well take something really worth taking; and something which would be no trouble to cook; and obviously for that sort of purpose the ideal thing was alcohol. So they went for alcohol. (The idea that beer is a perfectly good substitute for food is very widespread in the services). But unlimited alcohol without any food is pretty sure to get people excited and break down their inhibitions, especially those relating to the laws of property.

"It is an interesting theory that the naval and military authorities should not have granted the rather large number of leaves that caused the presence of such a mass of service men on the great day. But it must be remembered that the naval and

111

military authorities had no idea that the civilian restaurant workers were going to close the restaurants and leave the service men to starve. In fact, they probably thought they were conferring a benefit on Halifax by sending in a small army of servicemen who would have been only too delighted to buy meals at the somewhat fancy prices that the Haligonians have been charging, and would thus have put a lot of money in circulation in Halifax. In ordinary times, said the old Haligonian, the people of Halifax are just as keen about the odd dollar and a quarter as any other Canadians.

"The Service men, the old Haligonian thought, had no great affection for Halifax. There was no reason why they should have. In peace it was a small port town very much run by the Big Merchant class, who are very rich, and very much not run by the Proletariat, who are very poor. (The illegitimacy rate of Nova Scotia is precisely 60% above the average for the rest of Canada, pre-war, but whether the responsibility for this rests with the Merchants or the Proletariat, or whether they cooperate, the statistics do not tell us.) It gets along nicely in peace time under these conditions, but when war comes along and it is suddenly converted into one of the great ports of the world it does not adjust itself to the change with that elasticity and promptitude which would be desirable. In fact it continues to be a small port town, with a way of life, and a set of by-laws, very much unlike those of the other great maritime municipalities. After all, it would be unreasonable to expect a place to turn into a Liverpool or a Glasgow or even a Montreal, just because it was doing the shipping business of a place like that, when next year it will be back doing the ordinary business of Halifax.

"Take for example the business of purveyed alcohol beverages. In small port towns such beverages either are not purveyed at all, as for example in Portland, Maine, or are purveyed in the bottle, which the purchaser takes home and consumes in privacy. This is not at all a satisfactory method for sailors and soldiers who have no home and no place to consume in, and in Liverpool, Glasgow and Montreal soldiers and sailors are provided with places where they can purchase alcoholic beverages and consume them on the spot with their feet on a rail or their elbows on a table. But Halifax never got round to providing such places, and in a year or two will probably not need them. In the meanwhile however the service men did find it a bit inhospitable.

"But the old Haligonian was convinced that there was no element of revenge in the riot. It was much too good-tempered for that, and besides the rioters showed no sign of animosity against a particular establishment which they suspect of robbing their fellows, for a couple of weeks, and being quite nasty about it. They are not capable of holding a grudge against a whole town for a couple of years. As for the sentences on the convicted looters, the old Haligonian didn't see how they could reasonably have been much lighter. You can't admit officially and publicly that looting in one's own country is not a serious crime, especially when committed while wearing the King's uniform. Privately you could remit the sentences as soon as you felt that the ends of justice had been served, and he suspected this would not be long."

Nothing could have been calculated to more agitate the Eastern Canadian mind than such ill-researched claptrap and W. A. Hart, Chairman of the Halifax Branch of the Canadian Restaurant Association, lost no time in writing to Editor Sandwell, protesting the calumny in no uncertain terms. "Did you ever hear?" he demanded of the Halifax waitresses who had to stand by and witness an exhibition of Canadian manhood at its worst? We fear not, but suggest that you ask some questions. Halifax Restaurants are not ashamed of their wartime record, but proud of it!" To add weight to his denunciation, he enclosed a specimen menu featuring meals 'ranging in price from thirty-five cents for a two-course to $1.00 for a three-course meal that featured grilled sirloin steak.'

Halifax Editors, only moments behind, hurled themselves at the brash Upper-Canadian slander: "A Canadian weekly (on its own admission 'The Canadian Weekly') devotes most of its space and energies to running the gamut from symphonic snobbery through the parlor-pinkism to world-umpiring. So long as it confines itself to its favorite pastimes there will be few to complain, but when it sticks its aristocratic nose into realistic situations about which it knows nothing the complaints will be loud and insistent. In this case, the Halifax V-E Day riots ... which, according to this Central Canadian weekly 'wasn't a riot really ... merely a disorderly celebration.'

"The judicial inquiry into the causes, circumstances and results of the V-E Day rioting opened on May 17th — and on May 26th, *The Canadian Weekly*' appeared with an article 'Who's really to blame for the Halifax Riot?' and proceeding (to its own satisfaction) to indicate 'the real authors of the trouble.' And that, be very sure, comes close to contempt of court.

"People who know the facts will describe this article as cheap, insulting, patronizing, facetious, a farrago of nonsense and bad taste — and utterly and ignorantly untrue ... No Haligonian, old or young, who saw what happened, would promote such a tissue of insults and untruths. ... a publication that patronizes and talks down to little publications. But the little publications of this Dominion, by and large, have too profound an understanding of national duty to permit them to indulge in provocative utterances and puerilities!"

The Star Editor was no less incensed: 'Vulgar Exhibitions'. "It appears in an article displaying all the editor doesn't know about this National Port city and the V-E Day riots ... about as vulgar and insulting as anything spleen or bad taste could set down on paper ... and it is printed, not in some pornographic, fly-by-night abomination, but in that 'aristocrat' of the Press of Canada, Toronto Saturday Night.

"What have the business people of this City and Province — or the 'proletariat' — done to the Editor of Saturday Night that he should perpetrate such a monstrosity? Either he is grossly ignorant of Halifax and Nova Scotian conditions, or he is deliberately printing insulting passages. The idea that this City is 'run by the Big Merchants' is absurd — chiefly because there are no 'big merchants'.

"That 'illegitimacy' fling was, of course, dragged in by the heels to allow the editor of Saturday Night to exercise his lame wit. And now that he has exercised it, he should be thoroughly ashamed of himself. But perhaps Saturday Night is going in for that sort of stuff these days ... In competition, shall we say, with a type of sheet that 'decorates' some newsstands — until the police catch up with it."

Stung to the quick, but possibly against his better judgement, Sandwell unwisely rose to the bait and dashed off a rebuttal:

"It was not I who inferred that the illegitimacy rate of Nova Scotia was the highest in the Dominion. It was the Dominion Statistician who, in the Canada Year Book, 1942 gives the following percentages of illegitimate to total live births for the years 1938, 1939, 1940:

Nova Scotia  6.4, 6.3, 6.9

Dominion     4., 3.9, 3.9

I should add that the figures for all the other provinces are given and if it is any consolation to you, the next in line are Prince Edward Island and Ontario, practically equal."

B. K. Sandwell

Still another Halifax editor put it:

"This may be a 'small port town' in the eyes of the 'shoal-water skippers' of Lake Ontario, the 'canoe-minded gentry' who make 'seaports' of river-banks and lake-shores. No one is going to complain overmuch about their attitudes. Nor does any sensible Canadian imagine that mere sizes is the alpha and omega of community ambition. But this is one of the world's finest natural harbors, with a sizeable population living about its littoral. ... It is a port that should be the pride of Canada, as a national port, and an asset of great value to this Dominion ... What is that editor, his paper, doing to give this great port its proper place in the national picture, the national economy? ... To refer in patronizing terms to Halifax as a 'small port town' is to reveal a parochial attitude, a 'village' attitude in the person and the paper responsible. One expects these attitudes in children and the very young and ill-informed, but not in a paper that styles itself 'national' in outlook and circulation. ... It stands as a WARNING to the rest of the country, to the rest of the outlying provinces in particular."

Much chastened, the unhappy editor who had opened Pandora's Box beat a hasty retreat, conceding that 'had a more cautious editorial judgement been exercised ... the article might not have been published.' If Toronto Saturday night had not done its homework, that could not be said for another scribe who turned up the fact that Sandwell, along with Cardinal Wolsey, had been born at Ipswich, an ancient port community on the Suffolk coast of England:

> "Ipswich was old when Halifax was young. But Halifax (founded in 1749) was a well-established community when what is now Toronto was a bit of a village; when large parts of this country were over-run with wolves and aborigines ... Ispwich in England has a population about equal to the normal population of Halifax. Would the patronizing Mr. Sandwell call Ipswich a 'small port town' — of no particular merit or consequence?"

It became known that the Commission had asked *Saturday Night* for evidence on which the offensive article had been based. Mr. Sandwell referred vaguely to news dispatches and photographs, as well as 'a number of letters from relatives of men in Halifax'; the rest, it admitted, was theory. But when the Commission formally demanded 'the letters', Sandwell had to admit that there was only one, and that communicated 'in confidence' involving 'journalistic secrecy'. That term was new to Justice Kellock who, when he had read 'the letter' found nothing useful. When he returned to Halifax, late at night after the adjournment, he was greeted by a phalanx of reporters clamouring for his statement as to whether or not he would subpoena the wretched Upper Canadian Editor and bring him to the dock of Justice. "No comments," he said brusquely keeping still alive the pleasant prospect of a good pillorying. Later, Justice Kellock dismissed *Saturday Night's* contribution with a humiliating 'no value at all," and the incident expired with some local huffing and puffing about the scandalmongers being 'shown up'. Diligent research has failed to uncover a single instance where B. K. Sandwell wrote or uttered the word 'Halifax' again.

But the bitterness aroused in the breasts of Maritimers generally and Haligonians particularly has not yet been assuaged. Upper Canadians and especially those from 'Hogtown' as Toronto is widely called, are not all that highly thought of in the provinces by the sea. Neither is there all that need to wonder why!

Nor were men of the cloth remiss in defending the good name of Halifax. The Rev. W. W. Clarkson, Rector of St. Mark's Anglican Church dwelt on what editorials described as 'the heart of the matter' in an address titled 'Windows', the way "merchants advertise by displaying their merchandise in an attractive manner." In order to change and enlighten the people of the rest of the Dominion as to their ideas of Halifax, something must be said of the city in the way of 'Window Display'. "If I have to say anything about the rest of Canada, I address them as Upper Canadians, but what they address us as isn't fit to print."

"The people of Halifax," he said, "have had a hard time trying to dispense their hospitality for service men during this war. We are not a rich populace, nor are we spectacular in any form, we are just plain, honest, hard-working people who have lent our very lives for the existence of this Dominion during the trials of war ... It is alright," he thundered, "for the people of Toronto and other cities to talk viciously about Halifax, but if they had the influx of service men to tend with then they would realize what we have come through. If the boys overseas had to depend on Toronto like they have depended on Halifax, and the part it played as a port during the conflict, Mr. Goebbels would have been in Casa Loma today."

"Newspapers across Canada," he maintained, "have printed ignoramous untruths about Halifax. Some have gone so far as to claim that the people of this city took service men into their homes not solely for hospitable purposes but mainly for their money ... ignorant liars!"

Much of this sort of denunciation fell on the amazed ears of 'Upper Canadians' who had not had the least idea that they were so unloved elsewhere. *The Toronto Star,* rarely missing the chance to play the disturber role, reprinted Wm. Rand's feature article in the *Halifax Chronicle* for the edification of its readers:

"It is a rare occurrence in the psychology of war that a people who have been protected open the floodgates of blackguardism upon a Province and a city which has stood on guard for them, and borne the whole potential shock, with all that it implies, while a type of Ontario weasel, mingling with an occasional prairie gopher, dart down to the sight and smell of salt water, which frightens them, and scuttle back to the safety of their holes in Canada to give its press their inspiration.

"It is usual to assume that rebuke for moral delinquency shall come from clean hands, but it is amazing that the head and front of these attacks come from the City of Toronto, noted between the two oceans as the fountain of pulpwood literature. The vulgar avalanche, the mutilation of the King's English, the effluent of their crabbed press, unchaste in motive and obscence by implication, their covers great daubs of red, yellow, green and nondescript, caricaturing the human countenance till it resembles a Gorgon's head: it is from the habitat of this thing two thousand miles from danger, and further than that from any knowledge of facts, that the Maritimes are attacked. Practically the whole of this literature is domiciled in the U. S., but how to get it over the line into Canada is solved by the helping hand of Toronto. The process is a complication of tariff juggline, 'boiler plate' importation, set in an environment of sordid ethics which will print anything for a dollar.

"The observant reader can see, sticking out through all the utterances of the Toronto Press, the spirit of jealousy of the Maritimes and, in particular, of the province and port of Nova Scotia and Halifax. It is the mean spirit which refuses to admit the fact that it had to rely upon the Maritimes for protection, that Halifax was their only naval base on the north half of this continent from which sailed the vast argosies laden with the sinews of war without which Toronto would be at its wailing wall in the draperies of sackcloth and ashes. The Canadian war materials would be standing in dumps, useless.

"And this is not the whole story of Toronto. The reputable American press is today warning the public against the orgy of lying, fraud and fakerism of the bogus mining companies with which the city is infested. 'Keep away from

118

Toronto' is the motto, 'or you will be like the man who went down to Jericho and fell among thieves, and you will find nobody to pick you up, the only picking will be your pockets.' And this is the typical 'Canadianism' which throws its stink-bombs at the ports which have defended it, and of which Maritimers are asked to sing on July 1st, but who blow their noses and indulge in profanity instead. It is quite time that the thick-walled mentality of Ontario should be told where it fits, and that its congenital hypocrisy and bombast should receive from the Maritimes that which it had been asking for."

From Maclean's 'Parade', reprinted from the *Chronicle-Star:* "Reliable Air Force Corporal & working wife, both reasonably devoid objectionable Torontoisms, desire housekeeping room with understanding Haligonians. Morally, financially solvent. Will produce impeccable references, if incredulous. Housebroken, temperate, literate, desperate. You just might be agreeably surprised."

There was, throughout the Maritimes, considerable nodding of agreement with the sharp-tongued William Rand of Canning, N. S.

# Chapter 15

# WHAT THE NAVY DIDN'T TEACH!

Mr. Power was first witness, the operator of Tram No. 151, when the Hearing resumed. "There were about 2,000 of them ... a mass of blue," he testified, "many of them holding clubs."

"Did you hear any remarks as to how the Navy would celebrate V-E Day?" Mr. Bethune asked.

"I didn't pay much attention," he answered. "It goes in one side and out the other. They say so much I couldn't keep it all."

"Like a barber shop?"

"Only worse." Laughter in which even Justice Kellock joined.

Chief Conrod, when recalled, testified that he had not known the number who had been sent out on calls as a total of seven subordinates had been involved in deploying personnel. When asked by Mr. O'Donnell how many service people were on the street, Justice Kellock had to remind counsel that the Chief had been speaking of 'naval personnel' which was not the same thing but Mr. O'Donnell criticized Conrod for 'guessing'.

"Or forming a judgement," interjected Justice Kellock.

Chief Conrod had not been born yesterday. "Both," he replied to the trap question of his concern for the store windows or the liquor.

Robert S. Roddick, District Manager for Famous Players had attended a meeting with the former mayor in which there had been hope expressed that the theatres would stay open. He had replied that it would be feasible with special police protection but had been told that he could always phone the police station for help. Feeling that the authorities 'did not realize what the end of the war would mean in celebration', Mr. Roddick decided that the theatres would not open and advised the Press. "No one," he noted, "had complained of this action." He denied that he had 'feared a panic' but all the managers expected that 'there would be more than throwing confetti', being worried about paraders forcing their way in without admission and creating disturbances. The theatres had long endured such incidents, accompanied by loud and foul language. It would take about 20 minutes to get the Shore Patrol on the spot and by that time the damage would have been done. "All the same," he said, "the Capitol Theatre had been putting on a free show every Sunday for about 1,800 service people."

Mr. Stephen A. Doane, Chairman of the Provincial Censor Board, had noticed naval and military officers taking pictures of the riot at Keith's from the top of a nearby low building. Justice Kellock did not choose to follow up that testimony. Mr. Doane also described cartons of beer being loaded into the khaki service truck with an identifying circle on the front, outside a house which he identified by number. Justice Kellock seemed disinterested in further revelations of that kind.

Mr. George T. Holder, a citizen of Robie Street told of watching Shore Patrol personnel issuing cartons of beer to sailors. "They seemed to be a catering committee," he said. "They had 'N.P.' on their armbands and I didn't know whether it meant 'no permit' or 'Naval patrol'." That was too much for His Lordship. "Will the witness be good enough," he snapped, "to say what he saw and not what he thought!"

Leroy J. Zwicker, Retail Manager for Moir's, Ltd. and owner of an art store, had seen Shore Patrolmen 'enjoying themselves hugely'. Laughing at the sight of the looting. On being asked if he had a conversation, about the day's events, with a Navy officer, he replied, "Yes, I did. That's why I'm here."

121

Mr. Justice Kellock broke in to give his views on the desirability of counsel doing their legal homework. He did not want 'a lot of gossip', he warned them. And, when Mr. Zwicker in repeating Admiral Murray's remark that 'The Navy had undone its good reputation', expressed his opinion that "this seemed an amazing statement," he was rebuked by the Justice who ordered that the witness "must make no comments beyond what he had heard."

Mr. Bethune brought forward H. MacArthur Wood of the prestigous department store who said that he had seen patrol cars and jeeps on Granville Street, "all waving and everybody in them having a good time."

"Did you see cartons of beer in these service vehicles?"

"Absolutely ... they were Navy and Army. I don't recall the Air Force."

"Were the persons in uniform?"

"Absolutely. Drinking in the vehicles and that sort of thing continued pretty well until 7 o'clock." His only troubles at the store had been with the Navy.

"Were they intoxicated?"

"Well, they could navigate ..."

"Had they been drinking?"

"Absolutely!"

Mr. F. A. Lane who had seen 30 to 40 Wrens staggering about had got "the impression that a naval truck had served as a beer depository" and was cautioned to 'stick to what you have seen and don't draw conclusions.' Mr. Francis J. Hiltz, a store manager, told of a rioter who had shouted: "Mackenzie King will pay for this!" at the sound of which sacrosanct name, Mr. Hiltz was cut off and no more was heard of that sort of talk. Mr. George Hagen, a plumbing contractor, had been at the Keith Brewery fracas and had seen Col. Oland laying down the law to a Petty Officer of the Shore Patrol who was 'paying very little attention.'

Lionel Shatford, perhaps like Cpl. Drope, was not enthused about producing his movie film of the riots explaining that they were at his summer home in Hubbards. With rationing in force, it was 'a matter of gas and rubber.' That posed no problem for Commission counsel but the public heard no more about them.

Col. J. D. Monaghan had met the Shore Patrol W / O at the police station and heard how his men had nothing to use but their bare hands. The Colonel had happened to find the apparent answer to their prayers except that there weren't enought to go around. For the Commission's inspection, he produced a five ounce hammer handle which had been supplied to the civic force. Possibly it had been used to good effect for Dr. A. R. Morton and his staff had been very busy with head injuries and countless cuts. At the police station alone, over 125 naval personnel had been bandaged while still other walking wounded were looked after at first aid posts in the Y. M. C. A. and St. Paul's.

Colonel Sidney C. Oland, the irate brewer, recounted his fruitless efforts to get help from Admiral Murray at the Garrison Grounds. At Keith's all he could see was blue uniforms and patrolmen claiming they had nothing but their bare hands. "In my opinion," he declared, "a dozen determined officers could have cleared the crowd out. Although Lieut. MacKenzie was there, he felt the Shore Patrol needed greater direction from senior ranks."

A very important witness was R. J. Rankin, Managing Editor of the powerful *Halifax Herald* and a man not readily intimidated by what he saw as Admiral Murray's failure to enforce discipline in Halifax. There, sailors had come to believe that they were something special and it was not hard to translate that attitude to a feeling that they could do no wrong; or, if they did, it would be excused. A little swagger (not attributable to sea time) crept into the gait of your commissioned officer and was copied by the lower ranks. It was an *'esprit de corps'* accepted, even encouraged, by the senior command, who themselves thought they were very little lower than the angels. The worst manifestation of this naval arrogance came to full fruition when Tommy Tar received his pay and headed into the bright lights to get rid of it with the maximum impact. Mr. Rankin had been fulminating agaisnt this state of affairs for some time and in 1944, he complained directly to the head of the Canadian Navy, Vice-Admiral G. C. Jones in Ottawa, who had sent a Captain Connolly to Halifax to investigate. It was this correspondence which Mr. Rankin was obliged to now produce:

Dear Admiral Jones:                    May 26, 1944

My main purpose in writing at this time is to bring to your attention a situation which, if not corrected, may become exceedingly serious. It has to do with the shore activities of the personnel of the Royal Canadian Navy which have lately become sufficiently objectionable to bring forth considerable public complaint and a substantial demand that the newspapers should have something to say about the matter on behalf of the people of the community.

I do not suggest that the Navy personnel generally is at fault. I confidently believe that the trouble-making element would be no more than say 3% to 4%, but that is sufficient to create a difficult situation. With a number of protests before me, I took the liberty of requesting the Public Relations Officer and the Shore Patrol officer to attend an informal conference in my office and I endeavoured to place before them the reaction of the people of Halifax ... we had received complaints regarding the public use of obscene language; the attitude of sailors toward unescorted women on the streets and, in some instances, definite protests about the openly indecent action of men wearing Naval uniforms. Further, I called attention to the fact that damage to property ... was becoming more expensive ... It is surprising to note the number of store fronts in that area that have been boarded up after the windows had been broken on numerous occasions.

The two officers with whom I talked advised me that they had received a number of complaints direct and they did not expect that mine would be the last by any means, but they regretted that there did not seem to be anything to be done. The Shore Patrol officer admitted to me that he would not like to have his wife walk along Barrington Street alone after ten o'clock at night, which I thought was pretty good evidence of the fact that they did not consider the streets safe.

I pointed out to these young officers that the people of Halifax are just as decent as the people of any other Canadian city and entitled to the maximum of protection against actions of this kind. I further pointed out that the same difficulty did not seem to exist with regard to either Air Force or Army personnel. Further, I suggested that if the local naval authorities saw no hope of improving the situation it might be necessary for us to take a hand in calling for this protection. The next development was a call from the Mayor of Halifax advising that Captain Armstrong had heard that the *Halifax Herald* proposed to publish a provocative article ... The Navy did not propose to accept responsibility for what might transpire following publication.

I telephoned Capt. Armstrong, taking vigorous exception to the fact that he should have phoned Mayor Lloyd, and advising him that any time he had anything to discuss with *The Herald* it would be a matter of courtesy to communicate direct. He said he had been instructed to call the Mayor so I asked him to convey my compliments to whoever had instructed him and to tell them that the place to call in reference to material going into these news papers was the newspaper office itself. I then asked Captain Armstrong whether the people of Halifax were going to have to continue to submit to the present annoyance because the Navy did not see fit to do anything to correct them. He said that was not the situation, the fact was that there was nothing the Navy could do. When I asked Capt. Armstrong if the men of the R.C.N. were not taught discipline he told me most of them did not know the meaning of the word. When I asked him if they were not taught respect for the uniform they wore, he said there was very little time for that in the brief period of training the men had before they were sent to sea. When I suggested to him that if the men could not be controlled while they were in the service itself the position was going to be pretty deplorable at the termination of the war, he said he hated to think what the situation would be at that time.

Capt. Armstrong gave me to understand that the Naval Administration Authorities in this Port have very little, if any, control over Naval personnel, and if that is so, I suggest to you it is a most serious and dangerous state of affairs. I told Capt. Armstrong at the time that it was a pretty sad picture.....I understand the Shore Patrol Force in Halifax numbers forty, thirty-eight of which are in nightly attendance at wet canteens, the Capitol theatre, Dartmouth Ferry, etc. Following complaints....of extensive damage it had been necessary to place one Shore Patrol Policeman on every car travelling Barrington Street from darkness until the car goes to the barns. There are left for street patrols, according to his figuring, twelve men. I suggest to you, sir, that this is entirely inadequate to provide proper policing.....I understand that Mayor Lloyd also has received a number of complaints and plans to take the matter up officially with the Heads of the various Services....Thus I thought it might be of interest to you to have the background which this letter contains.

Yours sincerely,<br>R. J. Rankin. Mgg. Editor. Halifax Herald

A sign post to the inexcusable arrogance of the high naval echelons may be seen in the salutation heading the reply by Vice-Admiral Jones:

Dear Rankin:                                    May 29th, 1944
I have to thank you very much indeed for your letter, bringing the matter of the conduct of Naval ratings in Halifax to my attention.
Unfortunately, I am out of direct touch with the situation now.
However, I am giving the matter my personal attention, and will have somebody there before the end of the week to look things over quietly to see what can be done.
I could give you an involved list of alibis and so on, but I appreciate all you want is the situation corrected with as little delay as possible.

Yours sincerely,<br>(G. C. Jones) Vice-Admiral<br>Chief of the Naval Staff.

By July 7th, Mr. Rankin was able to write, advising that there had been a definite improvement, that Captain Connolly, the investigator, had explained a "plan for making Shore Patrols more effective and for dealing with offenders, whether they are commissioned or not." In replying, Admiral Jones advised that he had "placed all the facts before the Minister and we intend to press this question till it had been cleaned up."

The only difficulty he foresaw was the feeling that the Police might see this as encroaching on their preserves. He concluded by saying that "you have done a real public service both to the Navy and to the country in bringing this state of affairs to my attention, and I would like to express my personal thanks for the manner in which it was done."

There were many at the hearing who felt that this correspondence represented vital pieces of evidence, directly connected to the cause of the great riot.

Mr. Smith asked the witness: "In your opinion was the calling of the Minister of Naval Defence and the Acting Minister justified?"

"Yes."

Justice Kellock thought it rather a pity that Mr. Rankin hadn't confined his calls to less exalted personages. "Was there no other naval authority whom you might have contacted?" he asked. "Surely," he mused, "surely everything doesn't stop functioning when the head is not available?" He had evidently forgotten the previous testimony by the complacent Chief of Staff.

When Mr. Rankin phoned the Attorney-General's residence, he found that Mrs. McQuarrie was another wife who was not helpless as a stand-in. The main thrust of his testimony, to the public, was not whether he had breached protocol by writing and phoning to the great men, but the fact that someone had been sent into Admiral Murray's patch, leaving what must have been the painful implication that the Commander-in-Chief needed advice to run his Command properly. What would Admiral Murray have to say to that when he was finally brought to answer for his incompetence? What *could* he say?

# Chapter 16

# "THE INTENTION WAS
# TO PERSUADE!"

But much more testimony would go into the record before Admiral Murray's defence. The drama of the hearing would build in intensity till the chief character (perhaps by design) should appear on stage. Some cynics believed that, by then, he would have heard the most damaging testimony and be able to chart his course accordingly.

When the Hearing resumed, the first witness was Commander Mitchell, he who had been brushed aside by Captain Miles. Mr. Smith asked him: "Is it your understanding that the Navy is responsible for the discipline of its own personnel on the city streets?"

Cmdr. Mitchell was reluctant to be considered an expert on that. "I cannot enter into a legal discussion," he protested, "but in my opinion I've always been told that the civilian police ..."

"But surely," interrupted the puzzled Justice Kellock, "if the officer has been taught such matters as an officer, then he has some learning in the matter."

Cmdr. Mitchell allowed that he did have some familiarity with the King's Regulations and Admiralty Instructions, placing his hands two feet apart. "A volume that thick!" he averred.

Had he instructed the officers under him on K. R.? "Well, not exactly instructed ... I issued instructions that the officers are to familiarize themselves with the contents ... They have a working knowledge." He did not define precisely what that was. "It is not my responsibility," said Cmdr. Mitchell, regarding the behaviour of men on leave. "The question is over my head and over my rank!" He went on to describe himself as "one of those peculiar Navy personnel with a certain regard for Halifax" and Mr. Smith's ears pricked up. "Are you then," he asked, "telling us that certain Navy people have no regard for it?"

"According to what the papers tell us."

"Is there a feeling in the Navy against Halifax?"

"On my oath, I never heard an expression of that feeling prior to V-E Day!"

"Why then, under oath, did you say that you were one of those 'peculiar persons who had a regard for Halifax'?"

Cmdr. Mitchell had a ready answer for that. "Why," he said, "the four Halifax newspapers have dinned into me what 'we think of Halifax'." He then declared that only 50 were "participating" in the riot. Justice Kellock was curious why he had thought he needed 100 to handle them.

Again Cmdr. Mitchell was not fazed. "Why to break up the crowd and get at the 50," he declared. "And to take care of any in the crowd who might try to help the 50!"

Dartmouth Chief of Police, John J. Lawlor, was a firm believer in using 'persuaders'. When he found P / O Duggan's little band with only their bare fists, he equipped them and, together with his own men, they had got the situation in hand. He had issued no particular instructions on their use but they learned by 'instant experience'.

Mr. F. W. Herman, Manager of the Dartmouth Liquor Store tabled the following statistics of losses: 483 cases of beer; 141 cases wine; 768 cases of liquor. Of the nearly 1,400 cases, the R. C. M. P. had recovered 275 bottles of beer and the same number of other drinks.

After the testimony was over for the day, Justice Kellock and a few chosen ones repaired to M. D. 6 H. Q. where they were shown the 'home movies' seized from Messrs. Shatford, Fraser and Drope. What they contained will never be known as no one was permitted to refer to them during the balance of the hearing and Justice Kellock's 60,000 word report contained no reference to them. We may be permitted then to surmise that there were indeed such 'revolting scenes' that they could only be viewed without harm by those with the strong moral fibres of Justice Kellock and his entourage.

Finally to the stand, Rear-Admiral Leonard Murray, RCN, C. B., C. B. E., the lofty and aloof figure whose name was on everyone's lips, at least in the Maritime Provinces. After some skirmishing, it was agreed that, in Halifax, there were 16,800 ratings from Chief Petty Officer down, 1,200 Wrens and 1,200 commissioned officers. Responsible directly to the Admiral was Captain "D" who had 104 ships with complements of 12,000 men, not all in port at the time. The Commander of the Port with 590 men to operate 16 ships, 67 motor launches with 1,200 sailors. At Stadacona there were 7,800 of whom 4,800 were in barracks. Peregrine showed 3,800, Scotian 4,700, Seaborne 500 and, at King's College, a further 500. Justice Kellock soon established that the admiral could give an order to anyone in uniform in his command, presumably although not necessarily in his own branch, as he was the senior man of the senior service.

In 1944, Admiral Murray had asked Ottawa for direction with regard to the eventual V-E Day and had been told to 'go ahead on your own', leaving him unguided but free to issue whatever orders he chose. He had not really grappled with the problem till February 1945 when he instructed all naval establishments to follow certain general lines to safeguard naval stores and equipment, dealing chiefly with the security of ammunition lockers, magazines, etc. Gangways and scramble nets were to be set out to protect those who might return in a 'semi-inebriated condition.' So far as actual celebrations went he hoped the men would 'mark the day as a ship's company, as brothers aboard', but he gave no guidelines (he had learned from Ottawa) so that each establishment was more or less on its own.

Justice Kellock found it difficult to understand why the admiral's instructions had mentioned nothing about damage to civilian property and was told that the subject was "very far back in my mind. I had not expected they would do damage to civilian property." He had warned though that 'duty watches might become non-existent unless made up from reliable ratings'. A 'citizen navy' meant by definition that many had not had time to develop a 'responsible attitude.' Such types, in an emergency, might "fade away."

"Desert?" enquired Justice Kellock.

"No, not desert."

"Desert their post of duty in barracks?"

"Yes."

"Get intoxicated?" Mr. Carson wondered.

"No. That's difficult to do in our establishments." (Muffled laughter).

Each Commanding Officer was obliged to report his dispositions and those of Captain Balfour of Stadacona were first to be considered. His chief concern was his establishment and its stores and he noted that 'not much could be anticipated from the average rating toward maintaining order.' Captain Balfour had little faith in his own 'main guard' and Admiral Murray explained that this was because the men hadn't enlisted to be guards but had been assigned to that duty and lacked both training and dedication. He would have preferred a more 'reliable group'.

"If the liquor stores were to be closed did you have it in mind that the men would not be able to get beer through the regular channels?"

"Correct," replied Admiral Murray.

"That being so then, did you think of the quota on hand, that it would not be sufficient?"

"I did consider it but came to the conclusion that I could not ask for special privileges." Yes, he had read that Capt. Balfour planned to hold a dance for his personnel in the recreation hall. But it was noted that the entertainment angle of it was glossed over although there was great emphasis on guarding against 'wilful damage and fire'. At the time, he had not noticed that point. He had said that windows had sometimes been broken on pay days by inebriates who had been 'somewhat controlled by guards, but not to any great extent.' This was a rather odd philosphy to be expounded by an admiral with a naval tradition of keel-hauling and

131

'flogging through the fleet', reluctantly abandoned, although it was quite used to running an offender with his rifle over his head, or a heavy pack on his back, till his heart had burst.

"Did this happen every pay day?"

"No." He did not offer to give a particular date when it had not happened.

"Not as extensive as throughout Halifax?"

But Admiral Murray had been well coached. "Not as extensive as I have heard in the evidence here," he said. "You had better let Capt. Balfour explain," he suggested.

But that didn't suit Mr. Carson. "No," he said. "I want you to explain, and tell what was your understanding."

The admiral conceded that some damage had been anticipated at Stadacona, but "we had given no thought at all to what might or might not be done by the men who left the establishment."

Justice Kellock continued to press. "If it was reasonable, and apparently it was to expect damage inside Stadacona, it was equally reasonable to anticipate damage outside."

Admiral Murray was properly humble. "Yes, my lord," he said. There had been no arrangements for the traditional 'sing-songs' in the canteen as they had 'very little faith' in that sort of entertainment. In any event, there were no song sheets and no piano and had one been obtained there was no one to lead the singing. After being in operation for many years, the playing field was not in a condition to use. The Recreation Officer had received no instructions, so had laid nothing on. There were basket balls, jumping horses, parallel bars and so on but not much likelihood of their being used on V-E Day. Finally, Captain Balfour had issued this instruction: "All Naval Personnel are informed that while it is very much desired that everyone have a good time, anyone causing wilful damage to either civilian or Naval property will be severely dealt with."

Captain Freyer of H.M.C.S. Peregrine reported that: "Behaviour will be stressed; fire arms and ammunition to be withdrawn; no bonfires; normal wet canteen hours. Shore Patrol trainees would send "wandering patrols through

132

barracks to assist ratings who are drunk, to prevent fighting and to prevent the molestation of female personnel." The sports field was also out of use there and there were no special arrangements made, Captain Freyer admitting that "we didn't pay much attention to that end of it."

Captain Robertson of H.M.C.S. Scotian reported that he proposed to have all hands addressed by the Commodore who "will stress the necessity of ratings protecting themselves from the consequences of malicious damage," following which there would be a short religious service. Commander of Motor Boats would have Commanding Officers muster their men, giving a 'straightforward talk' which would urge them to protect themselves from the consequences of malicious damage to H.M.'s property. Nothing would be said about 'malicious damage' to civilian property. "...ratings can only be expected to act in keeping with the example set by their officers. It is up to every officer to see to it that his behaviour is exemplary." No one perhaps imagined that the 1,200 naval officers, with the seemingly lone exception of Commander Mitchell, would conveniently absent themselves, denying the ratings their examples of exemplary behaviour. Of Captain D's 8,870 ships' personnel in port, 3,432 left their ships and presumably hurled themselves into the riot scene.

Admiral Murray testified that on receipt of these memoranda which had been read to the hearing in their entirety, he had approved of the proposed arrangements. The replies convinced him, he said, that the need for precautionary measures had been appreciated by his Commanders but to ensure that uniformity prevailed, he issued a three part order:

(1) Cooperation with civilian authorities, particularly out of doors where the Navy could come under public scrutiny.

(2) Bars in officers' messes and wardrooms, and wet canteens normal hours.

(3) Necessity for the greatest tact and forbearance on the part of officers and men of the Shore Patrol.

He concluded by saying: 'I count on the commonsense of all naval personnel and on their consideration for the feelings of those whose relatives will not return from the conflict to ensure that the celebration will be joyful without being destructive or distasteful.' In dealing with the order that 'tact and forbearance' should prevail and that no persons were to be apprehended, at least a hundred extra copies were made and it is a foregone conclusion that some of them would be 'leaked' to the ratings who would not need to be too bright to see that they could 'get away' with almost anything short of murder. In the event, there are those who will say that they 'got away' with that!

As Admiral Murray explained to Mr. Carson: "In any body of 18,000 men, there are bound to be some who will go rioting under the stress of such a strain....The intention was to persuade the men to desist, instead of trying to stop them .... This is my understanding of police methods. "Prevention," he added primly, "is better than cure. The intention was not to create offenses by apprehending men who might be wearing their caps on the backs of their heads."

Mr. Carson continued to read the secret document: "Should the patrol see damage being done by naval personnel, they will attempt to stop it, however, if they are unsuccessful, no further action is to be taken as apprehending a rating on this day may be the cause of a serious riot." Justice Kellock thought that was crystal clear. "Is there any ambiguity about that?" he asked. "Is there any comment you want to make?"

"Merely that an incident was not to be created."

"Even if damage were being done?"

"Even if damage were being done."

"They were to let it go?"

"That's the way it reads."

Justice Kellock asked if a requisition had been made for truncheons, and the answer was "No."

"Only because the information had not been received that they would be available."

"Was any enquiry made as to when they would be available?"

Admiral Murray thought that the question should be asked of Lt. Cmdr. Wood. "I would prefer to leave that to him," he said.

"But I am only asking what you know."

"Then I don't know. No request for approval had reached me." In answer to a question, he thought the other services might have about 2,500 on the streets as against the Navy's anticipated 9,000, the same as on any Sunday.

"That's a normal Sunday in Halifax?" asked the amazed Justice.

"It is, my lord." Having supplied such a spate of information, Admiral Murray seemed to think he had done his part and would like to leave. Turning with annoyance to Mr. Carson, he asked: "Have you another question?"

"Oh yes, I've several!" replied counsel, somewhat taken aback. "Did it occur to you that with the liquor stores closed on V-E Day, the naval personnel might get out of hand?"

"It did not occur to me."

"Did you think that they might want liquor or beer?"

"The same as civilians. I did expect the restaurants would be open." (Which served neither).

"Where did you get that understanding?"

"I can't say."

"Did you think it important?"

"I did, after I found them closed. I have no recollection of giving instructions to find out if they would be open."

"You didn't think the restaurant people might want a holiday, too?"

"No. They usually make most of their livings on holidays and I did not think they would walk out on us."

"It did not come to your attention that most of the restaurants had been closed on Monday the 7th?"

"It did not come to my attention."

"But did you consider what might happen if the supply of beer was not adequate?" (To keep the sailors off the streets.)

"I had not thought and I still have no thought of the bad effects of not having the wet canteens open." Admiral Murray seemed to be a past master at the art of ignoring the questions put to him, a faculty which exasperated some of his questioners.

"I was not thinking," Mr. Carson began again, "of the bad effects of having the canteens open, but of the bad effects of not having beer."

"I see no bad effects," said the Admiral with aggravating primness.

"The sailor is accustomed to having his beer in small quantities. Nor did I know if the Naval establishments had any reserve supply to supplement their regular supply."

"Did you have any meeting with the Commanding Officers with regard to entertainment on V-E Day?"

"Not as a round-table conference, but the way was open to discuss it with me at all times."

"Did you find out what each was doing to plan entertainment. Or did you do nothing but issue your memorandum and leave it to them?"

"I didn't find out in detail. The memorandum was as far as I went."

"Did you have any consultation with Cmdr. Wood....Now it is upon us — with respect to V-E Day?"

"No. In the absence of any report I was satisfied he was ready."

# Chapter 17

# "JUST 200 SAILORS INVOLVED"

Testimony had brought out that 18,577 sailors had flooded the city during the two fatal days. "Had it not occurred to you to cancel leave?" Justice Kellock asked.

"But there was nothing to indicate that sailors were seriously involved or even leading," said the Admiral, straight-faced.

"Could Lt. Cmdr. Wood not have cancelled leave?" he was asked.

"No. He could and should have known of the night's events but could not have closed the gangway." Only the Admiral or his Chief of Staff could have done that and, in his view, if anyone was remiss it was the civil authorities who had the Shore Patrol at their disposal.

"You still believe it is not sufficient to make it a naval affair not withstanding the evidence given here?"

"Not withstanding the evidence given here."

"In your view, should the matter have been brought to your attention during the night?"

"No, I think that in the light of the other responsibilities of my command, it was not a situation in which it was necessary to disturb me. I should have been glad to have known but I am not holding any officer responsible. I still approve its not having been brought to my attention."

"Then," continued Justice Kellock, "if Lt. Cmdr. Wood not having cared 'to disturb you during the night', should he not have brought it to your attention first thing in the morning?"

"Yes, my lord," said the admiral.

Again Justice Kellock put the question: "After reading what had happened, had it not occurred to you to cancel leave, since Commander Wood could not, to put a damper on the men till you had ascertained the situation?"

"No, my lord. Because I felt that the men were entitled to a V-E Day celebration."

"Would you still have let them go if Commander Wood had reported on the situation?"

"I would still have let them go, my lord."

Justice Kellock asked if it had occured to him to have Commander Wood report immediately after the May 8th morning meeting. "No. I was too busy," the admiral replied. He volunteered the information that Captain Miles had told him the Shore Patrol had 'covered itself in glory.'

"What's that?" asked the commissioner, perhaps not sure that he had heard correctly. "'Covered themselves in glory'? Perhaps we'd better hear about that!"

"Well, they had guarded liquor stores, dispersed the crowd from the Sackville Store and at Hollis they had been able to take control." Later, he told the Hearing that stopping the leave of those involved was up to the individual Commanders.

Mr. Carson came in again, "Did they?"

"I never inquired," replied Admiral Murray loftily. "They do very well by themselves (without my interference)."

"Did you get in touch with the Chief of Police to discuss the situation?"

"No."

Mr. O'Donnell could not contain himself. "Why not? Because Commander Wood was there!" he said sarcastically.

"Let the witness give evidence," Justice Kellock chided.

"I literally did not have time that morning," said Admiral Murray.

When he was asked if Capt. Balfour had made a suggestion about the men who had already left for the church parade, he described them as 'men of good heart and good will who had volunteered to go to the church service'. It can only be assumed that none of the counsel had seen service or had been in mufti for so long they had forgotten the facts of life. Nowhere in recorded history is there another instance when 400 men volunteered for a church parade. Mr. Carson, noting that 260 only had got back to barracks, asked what had happened to the others.

"They dispersed."

"Where? Did you do anything about it?"

"I presumed they had gone to their homes. but it was mentioned later that some of them had joined the people down town. It has slipped my mind since if I did anything about it."

"The officer in charge might not have had a chance to issue the orders," said the admiral when Justice Kellock expressed his belief that 'departure of men from the parade would be a direct violation'. When in uniform there is one rule above all others. One generally keeps doing what one is doing till ordered otherwise, not much short of marching off a cliff. "What did he call such action?" The admiral was hard-pressed to come up with an appropriate term...."Breaking away from duty...breaking away from draft..."Presumably it had never happened before in Navy annals.

Mr. Carson asked if "the presence of naval officers in and around the crowd would have had any effect," and the witness, well aware that there were over a thousand he could have employed, chose to misunderstand.

"If the situation was as described," he ventured, "I doubt if one or two officers would have done any good."

"I don't mean one or two!" snapped Mr. Carson peevishly and with some justification. "I mean a number of them."

"It would have been detrimental to discipline for an officer to get into an altercation with a drunken sailor," he explained, "that's against regulations." When Mr. Carson moved on, frustrated, to that great afternoon meeting, Admiral Murray told him that "there was some hysteria there ... particularly the aldermen." That was surely an understatement for some were 'fit to be tied' and would have ridden the Admiral out of Halifax on a rail, could they have done so. "The mayor," Admiral Murray concluded, "was finally persuaded that a curfew should be enforced."

"Did he have to be persuaded?" asked Justice Kellock, once again not sure he had heard correctly.

"Both I and Brigadier White suggested it," said the Admiral. The tour of the streets had been suggested by Major Crowell. "Everybody was happy," he told the meeting, "except the mayor and myself. I was taking a chance. I was still Commander-in-Chief and still fighting a war in the Atlantic ... I had been told of a police wagon being overturned and I felt the same might be done to our truck. The mayor and I had no desire to be pushed into the gutter by rioting people," he added with an air of defiance.

Finally, the questioning turned to his inflammatory statement to the Press on May 9th, in which he had claimed that civilians were in the van. How had he come to form that opinion? The information had originated with his house steward, Petty Officer Boyce. At the brewery, he had been told, there were only about 15 navy men involved.

Mr. Carson expressed amazement, "The information you got was that civilians led the assault?"

Admiral Murray zigged from the track of that question. "I was under the impression," he said, "that civilians were leading the mob," adding in a quieter tone, "and the service personnel were with them."

"What did Lt. MacKenzie tell you about who led the assault on the liquor stores, on Keith's Brewery ... and engaging in the orgy of window-smashing?"

"He was not present at the orgy of window-smashing," the admiral answered in that evasive manner he had adopted. "I had been told that three civilians led the way at the Brewery when the sailors were being guided from it by the Shore Patrol ... I am unable to recall who told me."

Justice Kellock urged the admiral to think hard. "This is rather important," he said, "because it does not check with some of the evidence concerning the assault on the brewery." With regard to his provocative statement, Admiral Murray said that he had decided not to issue one, "but when we found out that the head of another service had given a statement, the decision was altered. I had been threatened by the newspapers," said Admiral Murray and the attention of the Hearing even more sharply focussed on him. "They threatened to demand my resignation in twenty minutes if the statement were not forthcoming." Here was a sensational development indeed and the atmosphere was electric but Justice Kellock decided to cool it. "Are we much concerned with what took place from here on?" he asked. "I'm not sure, but I'm asking." Presumably counsel got the message and the topic was by-passed.

Justice Kellock moved on with a question which was to result in Admiral Murray's finest hour on the stand. To it he replied: "It is my belief that not more than 200 were in the actual disorders, my lord. Thousands were on leave but there is some conflict of evidence regarding the numbers who came down town." He did not explain wherever else they might have been but referred to 'the information from W / O Barber that there were about 150 to 200.'

Justice Kellock leafed back through his voluminous notes and looked up: "9,508 went on leave and you have a belief that a smaller number went down town and only a small number of ratings taking part int he disturbances. Upon what did you base that belief?"

"I had no exact information. I'm trying to recall... Would it help you any if I were to say that it was a comparatively small number?"

The Justice did not need to refer to his notes this time. "I remind you that you said '200'. Why," he continued, "if only 200 navy men were engaged and 237 Shore Patrol could not handle them, were reinforcements not sent?"

"I had heard that both Navy and civilians were 'making whoopee' together, and I did not want to do anything hastily that might cause bloodshed. I thought that any interference would have caused bloodshed between sailors and civilians. The 237 were scattered over the city by the Chief of Police and were also engaged in guarding certain places. The Shore Patrol had been dispersed by the Chief and were no longer in my hands." Why could he not recall his men? "One of the things decided upon at the meeting," replied the admiral,

141

"was to protect the liquor stores if feasible, and that course was decided on."

Justice Kellock had run out of questions for the moment and Mr. Smith undertook to cross-examine. "Did Mayor Butler not say that 'you had the right to publish your statement but he did not agree as to the personnel involved'? Is not that a fact?"

"That is not a fact," the admiral retorted. "I would not say he agreed, but he raised no objection."

"You knew this statement would be definitely provocative ..." Mr. Smith began, to be interrupted by Justice Kellock who pointed out that counsel was on happenings after V-E Day whereas his terms of reference was the causes of the events. Where was Mr. Smith leading?"

Mr. Smith was happy to oblige. "I shall submit," he said, "that the issuance of this statement, taken with other evidence, indicates a state of mind ... that made him incapable of dealing with the situation that arose ... the admiral was out of touch with real events to the extent that, even after the riot was terminated, he had not been in a position to cope with reality because the real situation had no existence in his mind. The admiral's attitude, based originally on wrong information, continued later in the face of correct information ... It discloses an unwillingness to accept facts as they reflect on the men under his command."

Mr. Smith may be forgiven if he nodded his satisfaction that the line of questions was relevant. "Did you ask any of your senior officers for their comments on the following day?"

"No, I was too busy tracking down offenders. And no, I did not try to get an appreciation of the general participation of the Navy. I had set them another task to do."

When adjournment was called, Admiral Murray stepped down with relief. He knew how to zig-zagg to avoid shells, rockets and torpedoes but these uppity civilian lawyers were another breed. And they were not yet through with him. What might lie ahead in the uncharted waters of further interrogation, he might well have wondered.

# Chapter 18

# NO LONGER IN COMMAND!

As the Inquiry entered its 14th day, the admiral told Mr. Smith that discipline in Halifax was 'equal to that of United Nations forces anywhere' and was promptly asked who had told him that. "I'll give you two," Admiral Murray shot back, "Captain De Wolfe and Lt. Commander Lucas!" The latter was not known to Mr. Smith. Under questioning he drew the admission that Captain De Wolfe had nothing to do with the control of ratings and hence was hardly in a position to make comparisons. Justice Kellock found his patience wearing thin. "Answer 'yes' or 'no' to the questions," he directed, "if you know the answers. Stop sparring around. It is a waste of time."

On the subject of the Jones-Rankin correspondence, Admiral Murray declared that the visit of Capt. Connolly had been unnecessary. Matters of discipline had 'been in hand for several months and there had been great improvement.' When asked if he had seen nothing wrong, how could he have corrected a wrong that didn't exist, he volunteered the thought that "there is always room in any organization for improvement." "Did you increase your vigilance, and punish ratings for infractions?" "No increase was possible," said Admiral Murray smugly.

The questioning turned from ratings to incidents involving commissioned officers and it was suggested that a hotel manager had threatened to take action if naval authorities were not going to act. "Is that the only case known to you of breaches of discipline on the streets by officers?"

"Every case was dealt with."

"Do you know of any cases — don't generalize."

"Offhand, I can't remember a specific case."

"Then the statement that all cases were dealt with is not founded on fact. If you don't know of any cases, how can you say it is on fact?"

"I no longer have the records before me."

Justice Kellock was finding the witness capable of testing the patience of Job, but in view of his lofty rank contented himself with saying: "Please answer more directly. We're wasting a lot of time. Did you ask Captain Armstrong about discipline?"

"I knew it," said the admiral, stolidly.

"That is not an answer. Did you take any steps to ascertain just what the discipline at Stadacona was?"

"No. No further steps. The matter had been in hand for months."

"If you had been working on it for months and the Chief of Staff found it necessary to send someone down, then something *was* wrong with the discipline in this place!"

"That's not so," said Admiral Murray. And when Mr. Smith asked if it had not occurred to him that civilian property might be damaged, he replied: "I was not dealing with it at that time."

"That's not what I asked! I suggest," said Mr. Smith to the Hearing at large, "that neither the Admiral nor his officers had any idea that they could control their own men."

"You're wrong," said the admiral.

"I'm not wrong," said Mr. Smith firmly, but was made to withdraw.

Justice Kellock summarized the pungent red herrings which the Admiral had employed and asked: "If you were in great fear that the arrest of naval personnel would result in a serious riot, did it not occur to you that their arrest by civilian police, Mounted or Air Force Police would be more likely to start a riot?"

"Just as likely. Naval men are not a race apart and are used to being handled by the civilian police," the admiral

144

explained. "I felt that naval personnel were entitled to celebrate and were going to do so within bounds and not to the hurt of the civilian population." When asked about damage which might have been done, he replied: "I'm not certain that they did." An answer which is open to several interpretations. "Out of 18,000 men and 1,200 officers I could have drawn sufficient patrols to have maintained order. They could have done it," he stated, "in a half an hour on Tuesday afternoon, but not without bloodshed and possible deaths!"

Mr. Smith believed the witness was indulging in hyperbole. "Because you were afraid of one death you took no action from 1 to 6 o'clock?"

"More than one death ... with between 200 and 300 navy men involved."

"You used the figure of 200 before," Justice Kellock reminded him.

Mr. Smith pressed on, "With thousands available, couldn't they have been marched downtown and tucked the 200 under their arms and have taken them away?"

"I had 267 shore patrol men on duty," the admiral answered in that unique *non sequitor* technique which so irritated counsel.

"In you position, did you think it your responsibility to sit by at a meeting and hope the situation would right itself?"

But the admiral was not going to be trapped. "The outcome of the meeting showed that we did not sit by and do nothing," he said, easily. He agreed that he had ordered no probe 'into action by naval personnel on May 7-8'. No officer had submitted a report on it, the Hearing was told. He had kept the canteens open to induce men to stay in barracks.

"But it didn't keep them in!" Mr. Smith pointed out.

"It kept 4,000!"

"But not the 9,000 who went on leave."

"The 9,540," the witness corrected him. "No, my lord," he agreed with Justice Kellock who had said, "But surely, Navy men, no more than Army men, do not leave until they are dismissed by their officers?" The admiral had to admit that he had done nothing about the sailors who had left the parade and had not enquired why the order had not been obeyed. Mr. Smith then put the question which was in the minds of many,

"Did you ever, in your naval career," he asked, "give an order which you did not see carried out or left unpunished if it were not carried out, until V-E Day?"

"No."

"But on this occasion you decided it was not necessary to investigate?"

"I assumed that my personal order had been misinterpreted," said the admiral, neglecting to say if it had ever happened before and how lenient he had then been. "The group at the Garrison Grounds had discipline as great as any under my command." Considering that 115 of them 'went over the hill' that did not seem to say too much for the Royal Canadian Navy in general. Questioned closely by Mr. Smith about his reluctance to assess the riot scene personally, he explained that he feared indignity to his person, not from the sailors but from a mob of civilians. "And that would have been the end of Navy discipline for 24 hours!" In any event, he "had other responsibilities — fighting the Battle of the Atlantic!" he reminded his interrogator frostily.

"But you weren't 'fighting the Battle of the Atlantic' from 1 o'clock to 7 o'clock!" snapped Mr. Smith. "You considered it dangerous as Commander-in-Chief to go down town during the rioting?"

"Not dangerous to me personally," Admiral Murray replied stiffly, "but dangerous as Commander-in-Chief."

"Did you not have an officer to whom you could have delegated the task?"

"The same would have applied. It would have been dangerous to him."

"Then on that basis, if applied all the way down to the junior officer ..."

"Officers should not enter into altercations with drunken or excited men."

When questioned as to Commander Mitchell's offer to take 100 men with sticks to stop the trouble, the admiral said, "It would not have been legal to use them as proposed. I do not consider it necessary for my Chief of Staff to pass on such a request to me. He was quite capable of dealing with it himself." From the testimony there were those who had little confidence in how Captain Miles would deal with any situation.

"Because the 'war in the Atlantic' was still going on,"

said Mr. Smith, "if the port of Halifax had been attacked that day, would it have been your duty to direct naval personnel on the streets?"

"It would not have been necessary," said the admiral. "The Army protects it very well ... But it would have been my responsibility to get the men off the streets and in formation."

"Were there any arrangements for the sudden recall of men on leave ashore in case of emergency?"

"There were no arrangements. We had not anticipated trouble of that sort!"

"Did you believe that the rioting had subsided by the time you toured through the streets, and that there was not much left to destroy?"

"Yes, that's correct." In answer to further questions he had no corroboration of Mr. Zwicker's testimony that the 'Shore Patrol were standing across the street, laughing'. Nor had he subsequently given orders for an investigation of the Shore Patrol. Spectators felt that the admiral was still unaware of what was going on when he said, "I feel sure that such an enquiry was carried out by officers not under my command."

They were somewhat mystified when Justice Kellock cautioned the witness that "there is no need of repeatedly explaining"; then the bombshell was dropped into the unprepared Hearing. "The Court realizes," said the Justice, "that Admiral Murray has not been in command since May 12th." If he was aware of it, the spectators were not, nor the thousands of newspaper readers who had been devouring the testimony as fast as they could get their hands on it; nor the hundreds of thousands of citizens across Canada who were following the disclosures with the most specific personal interest.

Something had obviously happened to Admiral Murray! But what? Had he been secretly court-martialled and discharged in disgrace, automatically forfeiting all the benefits and re-establishment assistance? Or had he been allowed to resign quietly, with his derelictions swept under the carpet, free forever from prying eyes? Justice Kellock did not seem anxious to assuage the burning public curiosity and certainly Admiral (or ex-Admiral) Murray was not giving any interviews.

# Chapter 19

# "CHILDREN TEAR DOWN GATES
# AT HALLOWE'EN"

Indeed, Admiral Murray might just have taken 'early retirement', but those who knew were not saying. The Hearing continued with Mr. Smith concentrating on the admiral's blunders of command. It emerged that some naval officers had made statements to the press without permission from their superiors. "Did you receive any such requests? Did the Navy have any internal intelligence system?"

"We've no Gestapo. Just the Shore Patrol and the records of men."

"Prior to the Rankin-Jones correspondence of last year, did you know of the existence of matters in that correspondence?"

"No."

"So it was necessary then....for the matter to be taken up by civilians to get to your ears the facts that were public knowledge?"

"The situation did not exist."

"Did you so report to Captain Connolly?"

"Yes, verbally."

"Did you satisfy him?"

"So it had been a futile proceeding for him to have come to Halifax since there was nothing to correct?"

"No evidence of damage to civilian property had come to my attention," Admiral Murray insisted stoutly, "nor has yet come." Possibly a case of the Emperor's missing suit. "If there had been dissatisfaction among the men," he declared, "it had been about the condition their wives and children had to live in — congested quarters and having to boil their water...Not dissatisfaction with Halifax or its merchants or others. Evidence of this," he suggested, "was the fact that on V-E Day civilians and Navy personnel had been making merry together."

"If that's the correct language," Justice Kellock commented sourly.

Mr. O'Donnell wanted to know about the search for loot brought back by the returning ratings and Admiral Murray admitted that he had not ordered it made.

"Was it not required?" asked Justice Kellock.

"I asumed it would be done, but I was hot under the collar myself, at the time," the admiral replied. When his memorandum of January, 1944, was introduced, Justice Kellock commented that it was concerned solely with the posture of sailors (slouching forbidden) and the way they wore their uniforms (Hats at the correct angle). "So all the documents were directed to a general straightening out," the Commissioner suggested, "not to what Mr. Rankin had been talking about."

"Alertness and the attitude toward people in the street," the admiral explained brightly. "I understood from Mr. Rankin and Admiral Jones that that was what he had in mind."

"That's not the sort of thing Mr. Rankin was directing attention to," observed Justice Kellock.

Questions were also asked regarding the admiral's alleged order for the infamous parade from the Garrison Ground and it was decided that Lt. Childs was the only officer who might be able to say whether the order had been transmitted to the men. "Lt. Childs is no longer here," said Admiral Murray happily. "He has been engulfed by the organization."

But that didn't faze the Commissioner. "We'd better get him here," he said. "I will issue instructions."

They had seemingly run out of things to ask. Perhaps they did not permit themselves, or were prohibited, from those pertinent questions which would readily come to the mind of anyone reading this account. Admiral Murray stepped down from the witness stand, feeling perhaps that he, too, 'had covered himself with glory.' He would have another brief session that evening but he judged, correctly, that he had already survived the worst of it.

Attorney-General MacQuarrie testified that he had "questioned the necessity of reading the Riot Act as long as the services were looking after their own." Before going to the afternoon meeting, he had phoned Captain Balfour at Stadacona and asked that officer if he knew the Navy was 'causing the commotion'. He was informed that '400 men were ready and enough to clear the streets' but could not raise the siege of the Brewery without arms, the use of which they were against. The A. G. was in accord with that. Mr. MacQuarrie had gone to the afternoon meeting where the Brigadier explained that he had no trained men in reserve, just a handful of clerks, cooks and tradesmen. He took the opportunity to point out that the Army was hardly involved in the fracas, sentiments heartily echoed by A/C Morfee for the Air Force.

Mr. MacQuarrie referred to the 400 naval men about whom Capt. Balfour had so confidently spoken. "Unfortunately," said Admiral Murray, according to the A. G. "some of them have gone over to the other side." In answer to questions put by Mr. Bethune, the A. G. said there had been mention of '300 men who would sweep the streets' and he had assumed these were in addition to Captain Balfour's 400. "I was not too clear whether they were talking of the same force or not." He was not too clear on other things, it proved. It had not been Capt. Balfour he had been talking to but Lt. Cmdr. Wood who at that time had been unaware that 115 of them had 'gone adrift'. There was nothing for it but to bring back Admiral Murray to check the mysterious 300.

"Who were the 400 men the Attorney General has been talking about?" Mr. Carson asked the admiral.

"The 375 on the Garrison Ground."

"Do you recall a conversation with me in the Nova Scotian Hotel?"

"Yes."

"Do you recall my asking what effect the parade had and your saying it had little if any? Do you recall telling me that 260 returned and me asking what had happened to the rest?"

"I have no real recollection but I agree that you probably did."

"Do you recall telling me that 140 stayed to see the fun?'

"I don't recall. If so, Mr. O'Donnell will have it down."

"He might or might not. It's in my notebook!"

"It's probable that I told Mr. MacQuarrie that some had not come back."

"That means they deserted the ranks?"

"Not deserted. I assume they were allowed to go home. If I used the expression 'stayed to see the fun', it meant that they had stayed to enjoy V-E Day and therefore had not returned to barracks." A little later, he admitted that he had issued no instructions for reprimanding those involved in the rioting. Nor could he recollect any instructions 'as to dealing with officers.'

"You would recollect it if you had?"

"I think I would."

"I want an answer to the question."

"I don't think I did."

"You'd remember it if you did?"

"I think I would."

That exchange was mercifully cut short by Mr. O'Donnell who reproached Mr. Carson for browbeating the witness who still maintained that the situation was best handled under 'the original police set-up.'

"You think that's an answer, do you?" asked the exasperated counsel.

"My forces were still at the disposal of the Chief of Police," declared Admiral Murray. "I did not realize they wished me to withdraw them."

Mr. Carson withdrew from the interrogation, defeated by such intransigent replies and Justice Kellock expressed impatience. "Let's get along with this," he urged. It could be seen that he was trying to speed up proceedings by steering counsel away from their meandering cross-examinations.

Friday, June 15th, was termed 'Naval Day' by the media from the procession of officers brought in. Among the first of these was Lt. Cmdr. Wood. "Did you think?" asked Justice Kellock, "when you heard of the Sackville attack of placing other stores under guard?"

"No, I did not. It would have taken 40 men to a store and I only had 133 available."

"How many," asked Justice Kellock, "how many naval ratings were involved in the disorders....in more than a minor way?"

Perhaps conscious of his admiral's testimony, the witness replied: "As far as I know, my lord, I'd say there were not more than 200. I only had a certain number." He couldn't understand where Chief Conrod had got the idea that there were 'a certain number in reserve'. It had not been till 'late Tuesday' that he'd had any report that the men 'were helpless with only bare knuckles'. Lt. Cmdr. Wood recalled his previous conversation with Mr. Rankin and was asked if he agreed with the situation as outlined in the letter to Admiral Jones. "They were not worse than they had been," he replied, having perhaps learned Admiral Murray's technique. But he lacked the admiral's stripes. "No, my lord," he replied when Justice Kellock said, "I did not ask that!"

Mr. Smith wanted to know if he considered the changes suggested by Captain Connolly had been necessary.

"They effected an improvement. They were welcome."

"But I asked if they were necessary."

"Yes." He testified that he had not ordered destruction of his 'treat them easy' order. "That was Petty Officer Duggan's interpretation," he maintained. Yes, jeeps had been removed 'to remove temptation', and he had not placed patrols on the Dartmouth Ferry because the men might have 'been tossed over for a lark.'

"Did you have reason to believe," enquired Mr. Smith belligerently, "that the citizens of Halifax would consider it a lark to throw a man overboard?"

"Not the citizens of Halifax — people living in Halifax and Dartmouth ..." (i.e. Upper Canadians)

"You would have been surprised," asked Justice Kellock, "if there had been a recurrence had 'Open Gangway' been declared on Wednesday?"

"No," said Lt. Cmdr. Wood. "I was not satisfied that it was over." It was true, he conceded, that he would not want his wife to walk in the streets of Halifax after 10 o'clock. That condition was caused by drunks of all kinds. It had been like that in the 27 years he had lived in Halifax. With that, he was released from the stand.

The next witness was Captain George Miles, Deputy-Commander of the Navy in Halifax. He could not recall that the cancellation of leave had been proposed. As it happens, Justice Kellock had evidence from a Naval Court of Inquiry which proved that Capt. Miles had known of it. It was the first time that the general public knew such an Inquiry had taken place. Some, for the first time, realized the double strain under which Admiral Murray had been.

"Did you know that there were only 200 sailors involved when you talked to Brigadier White?" asked Justice Kellock.

"Oh yes, I would think so," was the reply. "The navy," he went on, "had not tried to compete with other attractions."

"You were not trying to keep them in?" Justice Kellock was amazed.

"Not if they wanted to go ashore." He had no idea how many officers could have been called out in an emergency but, after some painful thought, estimated that between 200 and 300 could have been contacted, although they were not. He had received no information on the destruction of the Stadacona gates and considered a report on the incident unnecessary. "Children tear down gates at Hallowe'en!" he told the Hearing. Mr. Smith exploded, "Do you not think that naval ratings hacking down gates was somewhat of a serious offence?"

"Yes, but ... that would be up to the Commanding Officer to deal with."

"Did you not think the burning of a tram was serious, or have you seen so much active service that it did not seem serious?" the Commissioner enquired.

"Not at the time."

"Did you have an independent judgement at that time?"

"I agree with the Admiral," said Captain Miles.

Captain Balfour's main concern, he testified, was fear

of damage to His Majesty's equipment. He had felt no responsibility for civilian property as that was the business of the Shore Patrol, responsible to the Commander-in-Chief. He had arranged for a dance orchestra but, as Justice Kellock pointed out, if the news came in the morning, "you did not expect them to dance all day?" Available were bowling alleys and badminton courts and movies; although the beer would soon run out there was always the Dry Canteen.

"Did you think that would have been much of an attraction on V-E Day?" Mr. Carson asked.

"Not exceptionally so," replied Captain Balfour. Cancelling leave had never really crossed his mind and when Justice Kellock asked him "how serious matters would have to be to merit such consideration?" he gave that oblique non-answer which senior naval officers had learned so well. "It might well be considered," he replied. The captain saw nothing untoward in the canteen 'horse-play' in which 200 beer bottles were broken, light fixtures damaged and 39 panes of glass smashed. "A practically normal day," he described it.

Commander Johnson had not deemed Lt. Cmdr. Wood's report of sufficient importance to call Admiral Murray. He had questioned his own 'quarterdeck' and had been told that it 'had been a very quiet night'. It was also his belief that 'Two-Hat Wood' was not responsible to him but to the Admiral.

"He was in the wrong house when he went to you, was he?" asked the Commissioner, baffled by the Navy hierarchy.

Captain C. R. Freyer of Peregrine had done his bit; each man had been given a glass of beer and he had altogether authorized 5,200 glasses. On what the Admiral had described as 'short rations', they had greeted this manna from heaven with delight, thrown it down the hatch, and taken off for downtown Halifax. When they reeled back, Captain Freyer and his officers "were so glad to see them that we welcomed them back, some of them the worse for wear." The gates had been flung open lest their presence impede the returnees and the stores had been denuded of candy bars, chips and cigarettes, all of which were 'on the house'. In addition, a torrent of hot coffee was served to sober them up and, for those

154

whose queasy stomachs could keep it down, hot chocolate. Finally, a dance band had been brought together and it 'had kept going till the last man had dropped.' Twenty of Peregrine's officers had been despatched to round up strays and all but six were captured. Under lock and key was a large pile of loot, including furs, but no names obtained.

Lt. MacKenzie testified he had seen two people dressed as sailors wielding clubs, and earned a rebuke from Justice Kellock for his semantics. "Are you suggesting that people dressed in sailors' clothes were not sailors?" he was asked. "Then why not call them sailors?"

Lt. MacKenzie explained that in his line of work, he had handled persons kitted out who proved to be not sailors. When he came to the events at Keith's Brewery he had estimated that "300 sailors or men so dressed" were present. No one asked him where civilians had come by any substantial part of 300 naval outfits.

Captain C. R. S. Robertson, O. C. H. M. C. S. Scotian, testified that there were no facilities there for entertainment. He had used shore patrolmen to guard the Central victualing deport as there was 40,545 gallons of rum there. "My responsibility," he pointed out, "not the liquor stores."

Captain "D", James Hibbard, D. S. O., said that 1,740 men had gone ashore so anxious to get into Halifax that they had left before the announcement that the main brace would be spliced. Following the riot, twenty-one ratings had been apprehended with loot.

# Chapter 20

# NO "REAL REMEDY" TRIED

Saturday, June 16th was to be the last day of the Hearing, and Lt. Cmdr. Childs, the Parade Master, led off, testifying that the admiral had told him that he may have to parade his group down through the disturbances. He had later understood that it should rendezvous 'near the Police Station' with Lt. Cmdr. Wood whom he could not locate. Sensing a terrible demonstration of 'Murphy's Law' he had raced after the Parade, found the Army and Airforce segments intact and had them dispersed.

"What was the Parade supposed to do if the Shore Patrol did not turn up?" asked Justice Kellock.

"Go back to the Barracks," said the erstwhile Parade Master. He had returned to Stadacona and found that the naval section had come home to roost but no one mentioned that about a third of it was A. W. O. L.

Police Chief Conrod's call for help on the night of May 7-8 was traced back to young Sub-Lieutenant Tunney who had the misfortune to be the Officer of the Watch. Promising to 'do what he could', he had phoned the Shore Patrol Office but there it was known that disturbances had broken out. So far as he was concerned, no further action was required of him; but Mr. C. B. Smith was now indignant. "Did you not understand that when the Chief called your office that he was not calling you personally?"

"I don't know what you're driving at," the witness responded.

"Didn't you think the matter was important enough to contact someone senior to you?"

"But Lt. Cmdr. Wood is certainly senior to me!" said the Subby.

Brigadier D. A. White tabled his roster as of V-E Day; in Halifax, in barracks, 3,253, on lodging and compensation 1,236, in outposts around the city 8,319, somewhere close to half the Navy total but considerably better behaved. He had declared the balance of May 7th and all of May 8th as an Army Holiday and considerable efforts had been made to have the men enjoy themselves in camp. One group had paraded with an officer volunteer in a coffin, representing Hitler, following which there had been some 'free wakes'.

During the afternoon of the 8th, he had reasoned that eventually the Army would be brought in and had alerted Debert. At 5:45 p.m. he had ordered movement and had secured the services of 60 Provost who were flown in from Camp Borden, near Barrie, Ontario.

Brig. White gave it as his view that had the liquor stores been protected, the service police could have handled anything else. On being shown the instruction that naval ratings were not to be arrested, and property destruction permitted, he had neither seen nor heard of such a document.

Lt. Colonel Charles Clarke, head of Army Provost, testified that 120 of his men were on duty on the 7th and the full complement of 169 on the 8th. "Did you ever get an impression or a report that only 200 naval ratings were involved in the affair?" asked Justice Kellock.

"No, my lord." He had given instructions not to interfere with men improperly dressed ( a very loose term in service parlance — in the Air Force it could be the absence of a tie clip) or joining in the jubilation. But with regard to property damage, 'there could be no departure from regular practice.' Any service or civilian found damaging property would be apprehended without hesitation.

He produced the Provost Manual and cited a section which read specifically that service police possessed 'equal and concurrent jurisdiction', That is the police of one division were empowered to arrest wrongdoers of any other. Mr. O'Donnell, for Defence, had not been told that such a manual existed and it was said that the Navy was entirely lacking in this basic guidance. Later, Col. Clarke volunteered that some of the Provost Corps regularly carried, not 'batons' as they had been referred to, but 'billies'. "A rose by any other name," commented Justice Kellock predictably as he gingerly examined the leather-bound object which the witness produced. "Quite a powerful little thing!" he said. Colonel Clarke could not have guaranteed that the havoc could have been stopped 'by the intelligent use of the available force', as the commissioner enquired, but agreed that no 'real remedy' had been tried. He maintained that he had never surrendered control of his forces to the City Police, quite opposite to Admiral Murray's contention.

Justice Kellock had one final question, "At the Tuesday morning meeting, was any suggestion made or consideration given to the possibility that nine or ten thousand navymen might be on the streets with nothing to do except what the city streets could offer?"

"No, sir. No suggestion."

Air Vice-Marshal A. L. Morfee submitted that there were 6,253 airmen and women in the Halifax area, of whom 3,307 would be free for leave on May 7-8. Unlike other senior officers, he had been put in the picture about the Monday night break-ins. Wing Commander Howard McCallum, Assistant Provost Marshall for Eastern Air Command, had also given him the welcome assurances that airmen were not involved. When the AVM had heard of the attack of Keith's Brewery, he had immediately issued a 'confined to barracks' order and had instructed Group Captain McEwen to cover the city of Halifax and apprehend any airmen in the streets. He had also ordered a surprise kit-inspection of all barracks but was happy to say that there had been no loot. Finally, he had ordered the immediate formation of a Court of Inquiry to determine the role, if any, of the R.C.A.F. in the riots.

W/C McCallum testified that he had 194 service police for duty in Halifax and Dartmouth and, as soon as the

European news came in, had sent his Sgt. Major to Police Chief Conrod's office with the knowledge that all available personnel had been called out. During the period of the Tuesday riots, there had been an N.C.O. continuously at the Police Station, but no requests for assistance had been received. "So far as you were concerned, your men were at City Hall but they were ignored all the time?"

"Yes, my lord."

"What would R.C.A.F. police do if airforce men were committing property damage?" enquired Mr. Carson.

"The offenders would be placed under close arrest," W/C McCalum replied. He described how, when the curfew had been imposed, he had gathered a group of officer volunteers and, with G/C Ewart who had organized a H.Q. at No. 1 Release Depot (more commonly known as 'Y' Depot) had swept the city. G/C Hanchett-Taylor, of that group, told of going downtown with officers travelling in pairs. The few airmen they had found were instructed to return to barracks or billets and, without exception, they had immediately complied. No officers suffered any of the indignities which Admiral Murray had feared and in a short time the exercise had been completed without incident.

159

# Chapter 21

# A FAILURE OF THE
# NAVAL COMMAND

No government could, for long, have safely ignored the Great Halifax Riot and therefore a Royal Commission was a political necessity, but one wonders if it was really designed only to placate irate Bluenose susceptibilities. While the actual events took place in Halifax and Dartmouth, there is little doubt but that Admiral Murray's 'incident' absorbed the minds and hearts of the majority in the Atlantic Provinces. They had been much maligned and it hurt.

Citizens from other parts of Canada rarely realize that the Maritime Provinces are a special case and must be treated accordingly. For example, criticism of the mores of Toronto, generally roll like water from a duck's back. But unfortunately, many of those same people have no inhibitions about denigrating the cherished milieu of other communities. In some cases they are genuinely unaware that they are rubbing on wounds which are slow to heal from previous encounters. Be that as it may, Maritimers are extremely sensitive to vilification by outsiders.

That this phenomenon is still alive now as it has ever been, can be demonstrated by a trio of letters which appeared recently in the *Toronto Globe and Mail,* following a peevish account by Toronto writer Barbara Yaffe and quoted without comment:

"If Barbara Yaffe encounters a 'regional hostility' to people coming from Upper Canada, she need not look too far for the cause. Her own first reaction on arriving in Halifax was to complain to your readers about miseries she had had to endure here. She now cites Dr. Morton Shulman's similar tactless criticism of Charlottetown and the ensuing bitterness as examples of attitudes doing disservice to Canadian unity, but her own contribution has not exactly been constructive. We in 'lowest' Canada are only too well accustomed to gratuitous insults emanating from Upper, and sadly, also from Lower Canada. We do not have to pretend to enjoy them."

Joan Dawson, Halifax

"We share the concern expressed by Barbara Yaffe in her latest effort about the consequences of the perpetuation of negative regional stereotypes in Canada. We equally deplore the role that she has played through her column in fostering such sentiments. We have searched in vain in her successive columns for any signs, however slight, that she may have progressed beyond the style that characterized her reporting. We feel that we can speak for a large number of Atlantic Canadians who have been offended by the comments of Miss Yaffe when we suggest that her work represents all that is worst in reporting".

John Rogers, Munroe Eagles, Ken Pike,
Kingston, Ontario

"Barbara Yaffe has accused Maritimers of being biased against 'Upper Canadians' — a monumentally silly assertion. As two Canadians who have travelled throughout Canada and have lived in British Columbia, Ontario, Nova Scotia and Newfoundland, in the last decade, we can assure your readers that Maritimers exhibit a much more tolerant attitude toward their fellow Canadians than Miss Yaffe gives them credit for — or than Miss Yaffe herself exhibits toward her Maritime brethern."

James & Gladys MacPherson,
Toronto, Ontario

Some of this general feeling perhaps went into the briefing given to Justice Kellock, prior to his convening the

Hearing. He may also have been not unmindful of it before he sat down to compose his monumental report. He had, of course, an official transcript, together with his own copious notes to assist him. One could conjecture, if it did not approach *lese majesty,* that he was instructed 'to go easy' on Admiral Leonard Warren Murray, a favourite son, and a distinguished representative of the Atlantic Canada seafaring tradition. How else to explain his forbearance in the face of those evasive answers of which the admiral had become a master? One hardly likes to imagine how Justice Kellock would have dealt with Ordinary Seaman John Doe, had such a composite stood in shackles before the Hearing and had treated it to such fractious testimony!

To His Excellency
The Governor General in Council:

Following a long preamble, Justice Kellock noted that the sittings of the Commission "were duly advertised and all persons in a position to testify or to give information were invited to do so."

"Before dealing with the disorders themselves, it is important to consider the period prior to May 7th and what was in the minds of civilians as to the kind of situation which might reasonably develop and what program would be necessary to have ready to put into operation.

"What was in contemplation is to be found in written documents which disclose that, having regard for the number of service people in the area, it was quite evident that, unless adequate control were maintained of their personnel by their respective services ... disorder and consequent damage would be the result ... any plan to be at all adequate must be based upon two fundamental considerations:

(1)  The object to be attained must be in keeping of the service personnel off the streets, where if left to wonder aimlessly in any considerable numbers, trouble would be the logical result. Programs for the day, therefore, would have to be designed to occupy the minds and the time of the service personnel and be sufficiently attractive to make their establishments more desirable than the streets.

(2)    At the same time ... there would have to be available sufficient force to take care of any trouble which might develop.

*The disorders which actually occurred on May 7 and 8 owe their origin, in my opinion, to failure on the part of the Naval Command in Halifax to plan for their personnel in accordance with (1). Once started, the development and continuance of the disorders were due to the failure of the Naval Command to put down the initial disorders on each of the two days, May 7 and 8. Subsequently the insufficiency of the police forces, service and civilian, employed, as well as their faulty direction of both days, and the passive conduct of the Naval Command in allowing naval personnel to continue unchecked on the afternoon of May 8 without taking any steps to deal with the situation until a very late hour, when the disorders had begun to play themselves out, explain the length of time during which the disorders continued."*

Having said that, Justice Kellock reviewed the V-E Day plans, noting that the Army's included a continuation of its policy that men in barracks would not be allowed to stay out all night. "The fact," he observed, "that comparatively few Army personnel were involved in the disorders indicates that this planning and its execution were effectively done. Similarly, he commended the R. C. A. F., concluding that, "Neither in Dartmouth or Halifax were Air Force personnel a serious factor in the disturbances.    A few, but only a few were involved."

The 60 pages and 25,000 words of the Report naturally contained a lengthy review of the Navy's planning, or lack of ... "No one, in my opinion, who as much as glanced at the programs of Stadacona and Peregrine for May 8 could fail to realize their complete inadequacy."

In the third section of the Report he dealt with Naval descipline in Halifax prior to V-E Day.    "The evidence established," he wrote, "that vandalism, breaking of plate glass windows and tearing down of awnings and street signs, mostly by intoxicated Naval ratings on pay days, was a usual and expected occurrence.    Admiral Murray had held that 'it had not been necessary to send anyone from Ottawa as the conditions complained of did not exist.' But, he pointed out,

"The letters of the Chief of Naval Staff would not seem to reflect the same view."

Section Four dealt with control forces with 133 to handle about 18,000 (of which 1,000 were Wrens) normally rambunctious sailors. By comparison for 4,500 normally well-behaved soldiers, there were 169 Provost. With regard to the miniscule 1,000 airmen and women, the conduct of whose members was almost always impeccable, there were nearly two thirds the number of the Naval Shore Patrol! This was a curious situation for which Vice-Admiral George Jones ought to have borne some culpability, although no one quite dared to suggest that.

Justice Kellock outlined the instructions which Lt. Cmdr. Wood had issued ... "damage bound to occur ... little further action to be taken ... no person to be apprehended unless absolutely necessary ... apprehending a rating on this day may be the cause of a serious riot ... No charge will be laid for drunkenness and any naval personnel in the vicinity when the drunk is removed should be informed of this fact ... if he is with 'pals', who say they will take care of him, let them do it." The Justice could find no evidence that this order had been permitted wide circulation amongst the ratings, but observed; "I would think that it would not be long, after the policy laid down began to be practised, before the sailors would realize that they had very little to fear from the Shore Patrol. It is, of course, one thing for a policeman to exercise discretion where a carnival spirit is abroad and being exercised harmlessly. It is another thing, however, for the policeman to abdicate his functions in the presence of destructive lawlessness."

After detailed descriptions of the events on May 7 and 8, Justice Kellock gave a longish account of the 4:30 p.m. meeting presided over by Admiral Murray as the Senior Officer present. "Just where he received this information that 'a very small number of ratings were involved in the disturbances' I do not know, nor do I know how he could have received that impression." A little later, he noted; "Admiral Murray showed a similar unwillingness to accept facts in connection with the events of the preceding night, as well as in connection with the complaints as to the conduct of ratings on Halifax streets in June, 1944."

"Not withstanding the evidence you have heard here?"

"Not withstanding the evidence I have heard here!"

"The importance of this attitude of mind in failing or refusing to accept the actual facts of the situation ... is that he was less able effectively to deal with it ... it was not till the conclusion of that meeting that he took any other action."

Also contentious was the role of the restaurants; on May 8th, these maligned establishments actually served 7,897 full course meals and 3,991 snacks, pretty well refuting the Navy argument that the riot had been set off by a lack of food for the sailors downtown. The Justice expressed the opinion that "there is no reasonable basis, on the evidence, for the view that the Stadacona sailors harboured any resentment for the restaurants being closed or carried such resentment the length of smashing up blocks of business premises after they themselves had been well fed."

He also paid tribute to the considerable body of volunteer workers (which in fact included many non-residents) who had done much in the way of entertainment, recreation and welfare ... I have no doubt that individuals have had trying experiences in crowded Halifax as other people have experienced discomfort during the war in other crowded centres of population.

After showing for the Governor-General's delectation the great quantities of liquor etc. stolen from the provincial outlets, he recapitulated the damage incurred in Halifax by merchants and others. "In that city," he wrote, "654 firms suffered damages; 2,624 pieces of plate and other glass was broken and 207 firms suffered from looting in some degree." A short section was included, dealing with the activities of the Merchant Marine and he found that, apart from a few isolated instances, they were not a serious factor, a conclusion which would not sit well with those who had blamed "foreigners". In closing, he found it worth recording that "only 34 naval bodies were arrested on various charges, apart from drunkeness!" which of itself had not been considered a naval offence during most of the celebrations. After that, he did not think there was anything else he could usefully add.

It was apparent to many, having followed the course of the historic riots almost hour by hour, that there had been a number of topics to which he made little or no reference. The Report fails to even suggest the supposedly sensational amateur movies which had been shown only to a select few. As well, there seemed to be no mention of the death of a naval officer which thousands were convinced was a *quid pro quo,* but this was perhaps deleted in deference to the family of the deceased.

There are a number of items which remain uncertain to this day and we are unable to give accurate credit to that RCMP guard who first learned of the impending raid on "Oland's". Justice Kellock referred to the man as Constable Pitt, who was said to have passed the news to his superior, Cpl. McLean; contemporary newspaper reports indicate that Cpl. McLean himself had been the first to hear the warning from a sailor. The name of the Shore Patrol Warrant Officer takes turns as appearing as Barbour and Barber; as does Conrod and Conrad, the Halifax Police Chief.

Naval Minister Douglas Abbott understandably would not make public the proceedings of a parallel Naval Board of Inquiry, but did concede that "disciplinary action had been taken so far as it was necessary within the naval services", leaving us to conjecture what, if anything, had transpired. It is a personal opinion of this writer that Vice-Admiral George Jones should have borne some of the responsibility. Although he moved swiftly to answer the complaints of Mr. Rankin, the bold Halifax Editor, he did not know, and should have known (or did he really know and did nothing about it?) the administrative weaknesses in the North-West Atlantic Command, bared to public view by Justice Kellock's Commission. Its Commander-in-Chief was a brave and competent ship's master, but as an administrator the embodiment of the Peter Principle, for he was hopelessly inept in his exalted rank in a shore establishment.

It is understandable that the Royal Canadian Navy's blackest blot would be swept under the rug of the Naval Archives in 1945. The proceedings of the Naval Board of Inquiry are now held inviolate by the National Personnel Records Centre of the Public Archives of Canada. It is less understandable that, thirty five years later, it is still impossible to arrange access to the documents. According to the Hon. J. Gilles Lamontagne, Minister of National Defence, they are not even accessible to his own Department.

In seeking to pull back the rug, on behalf of a constituent, Mr. Douglas Lewis, M. P. Simcoe North, has argued that, "If Canadians are to learn from the past, then I would suggest that the past must be opened to people with a legitimate interest in history!"

A further request has been made to the Hon. Francis Fox, Secretary of State, Minister of Communications, for an opinion on whether the documents related to 'Murray's Folly' would be released to the public "in the event that the Freedom of Information Act, introduced by the Minister, becomes law." At the time of this writing, no reply has been forthcoming.

It can be said that Admiral Murray retired officially in 1946 and moved to England, where he studied Law and became President of the Inns of Court in 1948. He was called to the Bar by the Middle Temple in 1949, at the age of fifty three, and settled down in Buxton, in Derbyshire, full of honours awarded by foreign governments.

France made him a Commander of the Legion of Honour and he was given the *Croix de Guerre* with Palms. The United States of America made him a Commander of the Legion of Merit, and Norway presented him with the Cross of Liberation. But, in Canada, he was generally thought to have borne the major culpability for the Great Halifax Riot on V-E Day, 1945, following his 'Open Gangway' policy, 'Murray's Folly', which precipitated and then nourished it.

The summer of 1980 saw the Government of Nova Scotia celebrating the 70th Anniversary of the founding of the Royal Canadian Navy, with a spectacular Tattoo held in Halifax in June. On an upper stairway in Admiralty House, now a naval museum, a series of photographs of former Commanders-in-Chief are on display with the noticeable omission of the V-E Day admiral. One suspects that it was just as well that the spectre of a most disgraceful episode was not seated at the feast. The full story has yet to be told and there are those who believe it would 'open the old wounds', 'could still touch off a re-enactment of the Riots on Barrington Street.'

Midland
October, 1980

167

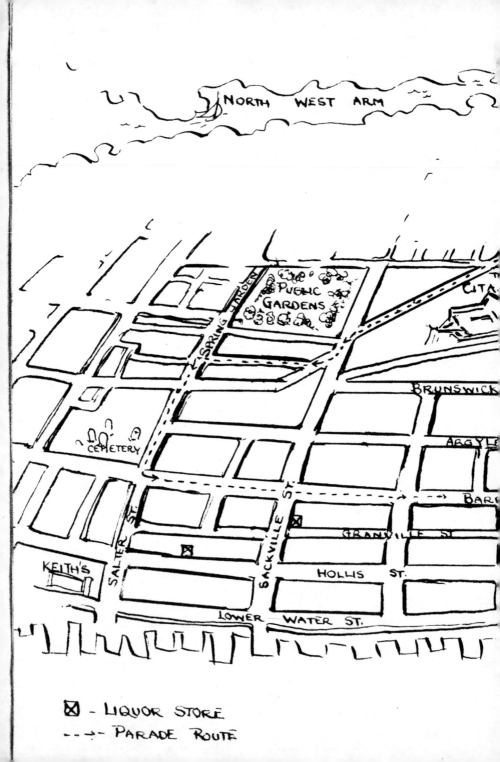

NORTH WEST ARM

PUBLIC GARDENS

SPRING GARDEN

CITA

BRUNSWICK

ARGYLE

CEMETERY

BAR

GRANVILLE ST

SACKVILLE ST.

HOLLIS ST.

KEITH'S

SALTER ST.

LOWER WATER ST.

☒ - LIQUOR STORE

--→- PARADE ROUTE

HALIFAX - 1945